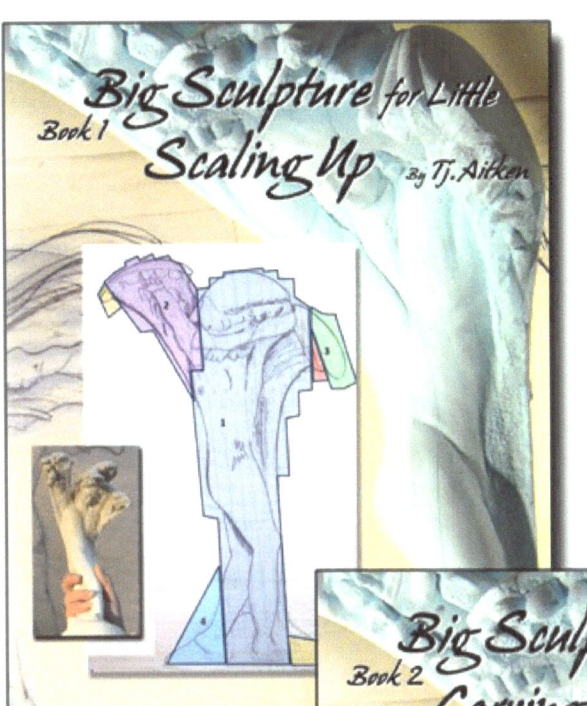

Big Sculpture for Little
Book 1
Scaling Up
By TJ. Aitken

Big Sculpture for Little
Book 2
Carving Foam
By TJ. Aitken

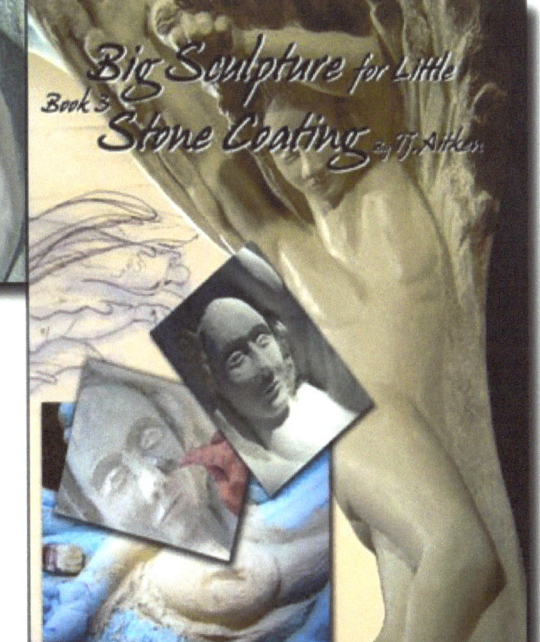

Big Sculpture for Little
Book 3
Stone Coating
By TJ. Aitken

Get the entire set, available at:
www.SculptureByTj.com

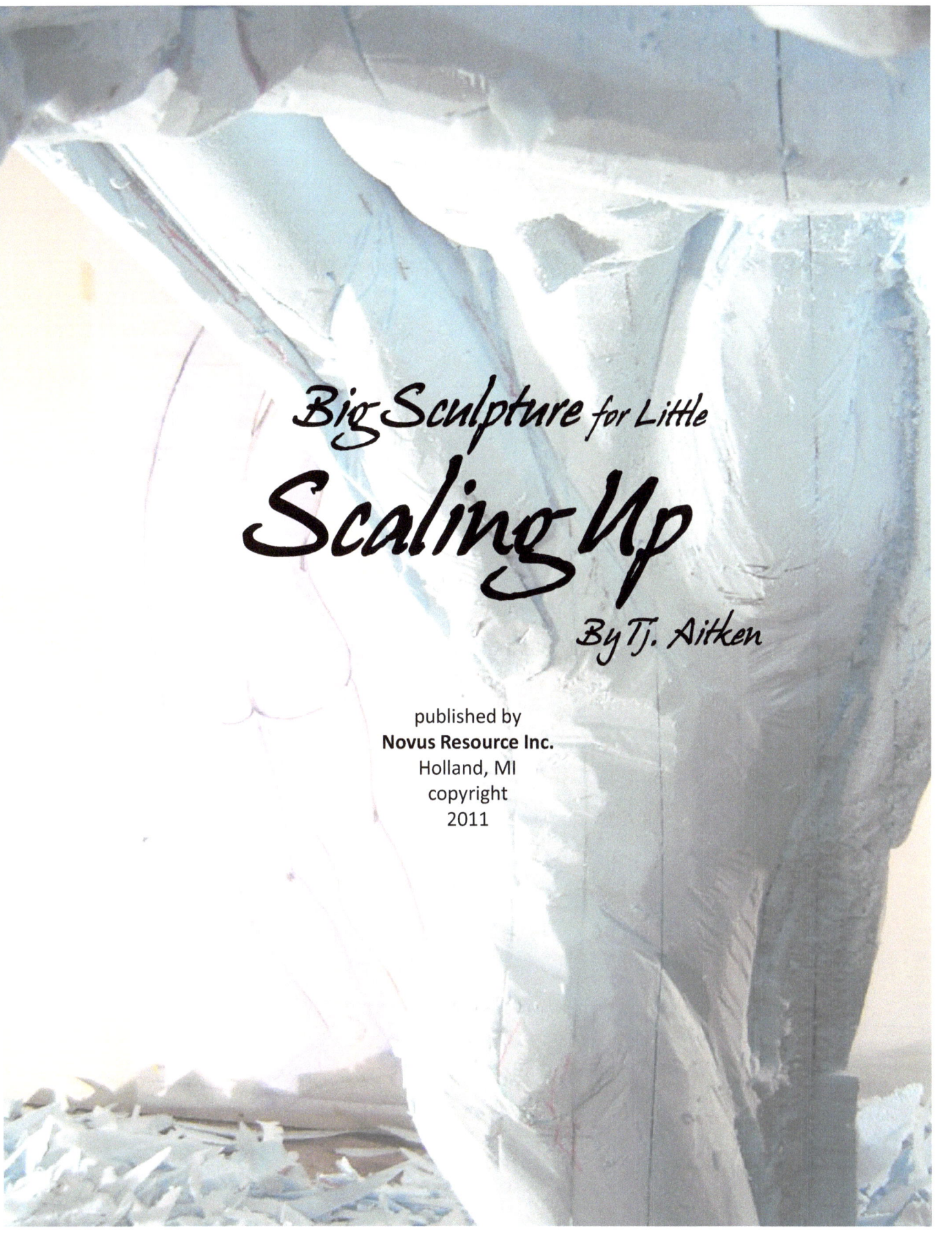

Big Sculpture for Little

Scaling Up

By T.J. Aitken

published by
Novus Resource Inc.
Holland, MI
copyright
2011

To the sculptor:
The 3 book series is a step by step explanation for creating big sculpture for very little money. Tj's studio photographs and notes have been laid out to best show the process he developed over several years. The text includes discussion on tools and techniques as they are used on the pieces, as well as errors and how to fix them. All three books are intended as studio guides for experienced sculptors who are ready for some new professional techniques. Simple, inexpensive tools and materials are used to make dramatic works. The final book illustrates the formula developed for stone coating the pieces with a new process using polymer modified concrete.

Content & Process Outline
(a summary for use on your project)

Preparation: Read the entire book and create your maquette while thinking through the full size build. Paint the maquette white and get a digital camera.

1. Working from Maquettes.   6

2. Photograph the maquette for creating control drawings.   7

3. Prepare digital shots for projection.   9, 39

4. Reconcile views, create the drawing from the projection.   10

     About Foam   14

5. Cutting Sections   15

6. Glue Laminating   20

     Viewing   25

7. Planning for Fixtures and Hogging   28

8. Adding Pieces– different methods   30

A Simple Project in relief to get familiar with the process   39

     About the Art   44

     Carving Foam- tools and techniques are covered in: Book 2.

     Stone Coating - polymer modified cement, covered in: Book 3.

Introduction to Scaling Up and the Blocking Process

We will walk through the process for turning your small sculpture into a large one and how to construct the Block from inexpensive foam materials. This process enables the construction of very complex sculpture, industrial patterns, and virtually anything you want to make. This series, **Big sculpture for little,** shows you a project all the way through in pictures. In this book you will learn the secrets to setting up accurately for the carving process, and how to use the least amount of material.

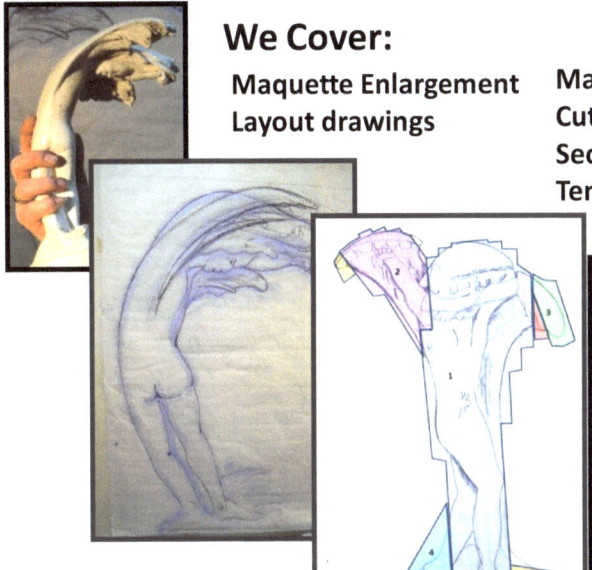

We Cover:

Maquette Enlargement
Layout drawings

Major block construction
Cutting material
Section work
Template making

Calculating stack up
Tools
Glue laminating
Supports and appendages
Strategies for construction

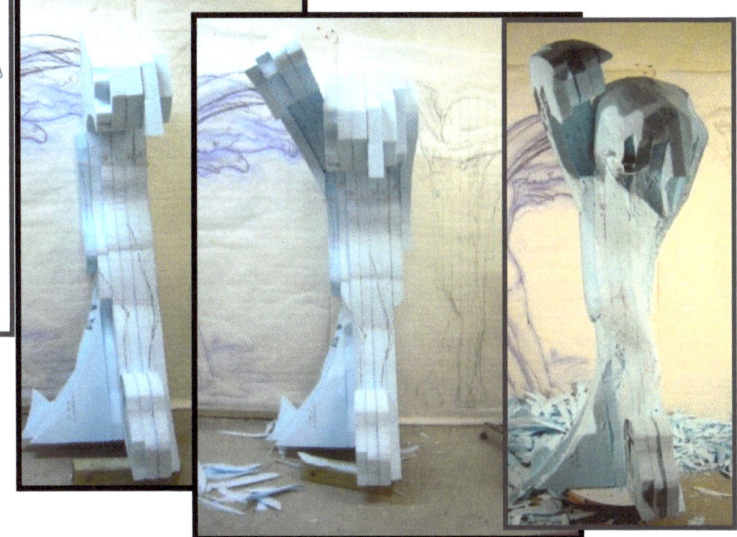

The rest of the series covers:

Book 2- Foam carving techniques

Book 3- Stone coating methods and materials

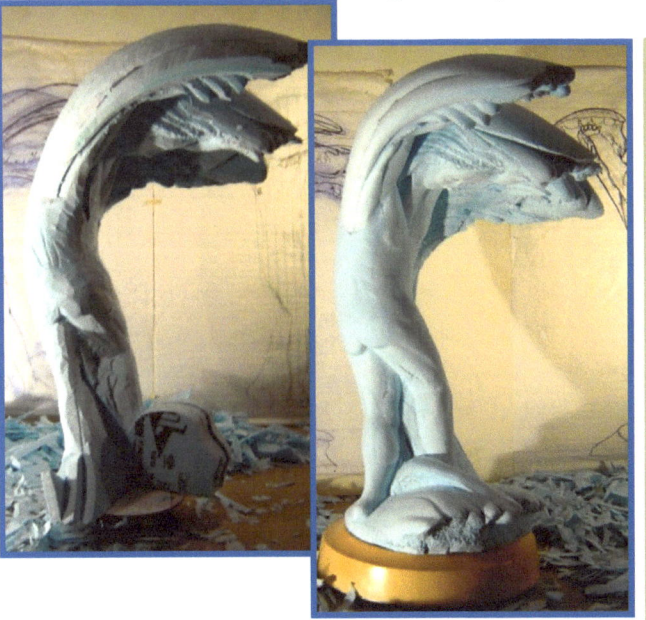

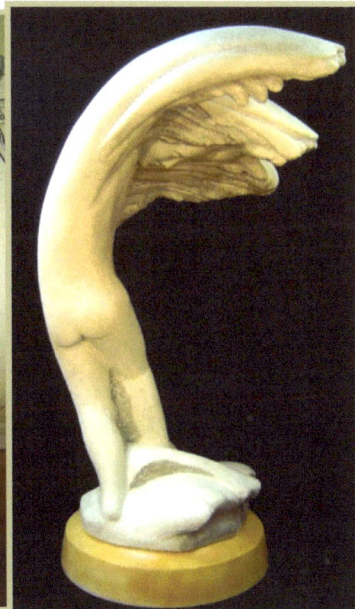

Working from Maquettes

If you have basic craftsmanship skills you can take a small model, known as a maquette, and produce an accurate enlargement. It helps to have had a drafting class. But it's not critical. If you sculpt you should have no problems with these techniques. If you have carpentry skills this process should be no problem. The piece in these pictures is an elaborate form. It was chosen because it will show you the complete range of what can be done with this process. If we can make this figure life sized in foam we can make virtually any other form we would like.

Why a Maquette?

We will be using a maquette all the way through this book and most of the way through the carving book as well. I highly recommend a small maquette on a large project. The process of creating the little one not only lets you design and refine the form but it allows you to think through making the large version as you work. You can envision the process, materials, problems of construction, and logistics of sizes and weights while you create your maquette.

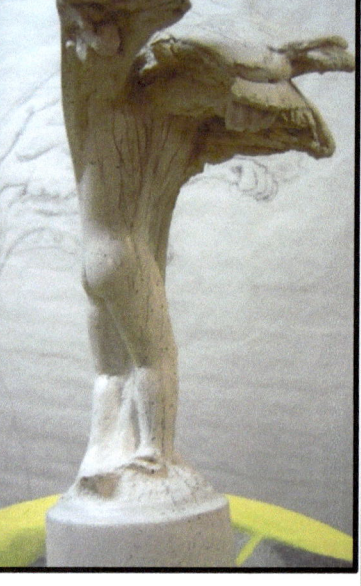

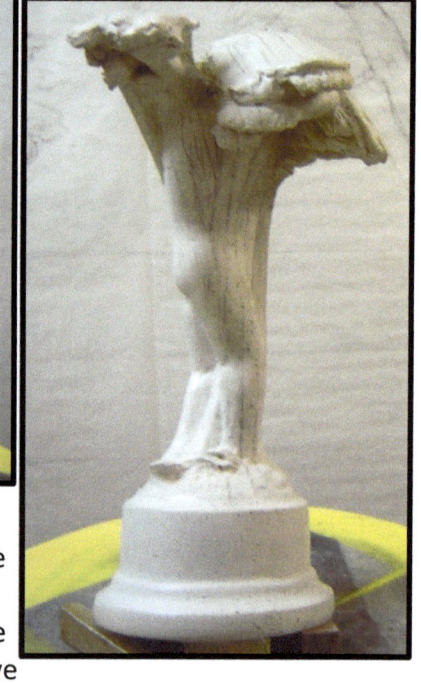

This helps percolate those great solutions that make the project go well. Sculpting a maquette is not covered here but it is assume that you have one and are ready to make an enlargement, and want to construct the piece from foam for coating with concrete. This one is a plaster cast. It is hard and white, allowing easy view of form shadow and drawing reference lines on the surface. I recommend painting your maquette if it is not white. Your maquette is a working tool, you will abuse it, so a hard material is better. First considerations are about the change in scale. Some things you can get away with on a small scale are not a good idea large. The upper mass of this piece was cantilevered too far for the life sized construction plan. Wedges were glued to the maquette to set an angle more appropriate for the full size.

The lines are scale approximations of the foam planking and will help plan the block we will make.

Maquette to Full Size Control Drawing - The Photos

You need to choose the two best views of the maquette for the control drawings
– A **Side View** for most patterns – An **End View** to show block laminations.
Here are the two shots used on our project. Below are the control drawings from the wall. Position the camera at mid height to see all the detail that allows you to do the line drawings.

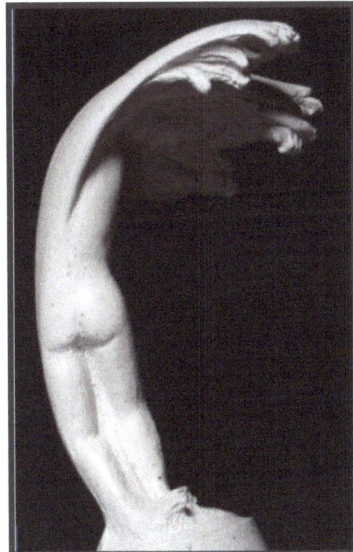

Side View

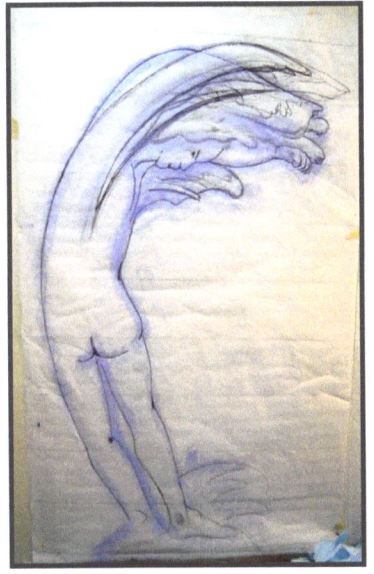

View selection is Key- The long arms on this piece will be strongest and most easily made from slices stacked in this SIDE view. All the fingers and wave detail are a natural for 2" foam stock in the END view. The photos should be simple and clear. You need to see major forms. Setting a single light source helps define edges with shadows. Seeing line is more important than beauty in your photograph.
Use a turn table if you can and get the camera at the same height and distance in both shots, straight from the middle. It is a good idea to get lots of documentation of this maquette in case you trash it in the work process like I did. Extra views help you see the form. Don't forget down from the top (Plan View).

If you know the PowerPoint program, it is easy to import your shots and set up a scale study of your control drawings. Put them side by side and draw horizontal lines at major details in bright colors. You can even dimension the piece in this program if you're able, if not, no worries, read on.

You will need to round up a computer and an (overhead) data projector. If you haven't gone digital you will have to make drawings by measuring the piece and calculating distances between points. If you don't have a data projector you could join a church or find a school teacher, art center or library that you can borrow one from. Most places like these use them. You may need to put your paper up where the projector is, so mark your piece height on the paper. It is easy to adjust an image to your new scale by using the projector lens and moving the

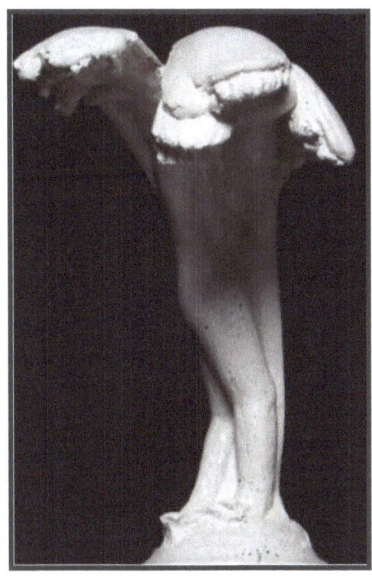

End View

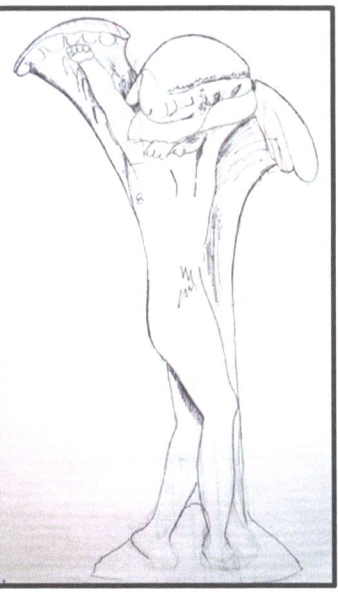

projector or the paper distance until it fits. You want your two views on separate pieces of paper. The side view will be used a lot for templates. Consider the lamination of foam planks and how the slices will join together on the end view.

One trick: If you have hidden content opposite your side view you can shoot a pick of that side of the maquette and reverse the image for projection. This allows you to clearly indicate hidden items on the drawing.

Enlargement from a Maquette
Creating Control Drawing Views or- The Layout

The layout is your map and blueprint for all the decisions and planning of work to construct this piece. A layout must have two views that are proportionately correct to each other and indicate all the key details that you intend to create. **Think of them as mounted to a block.** One on the side and one on the end. If we cut to these lines through the block we get a simple version of our piece. This is why we are so careful to get the dimensions right. The views are perpendicular in 3D but we set them out side by side for our layout work.

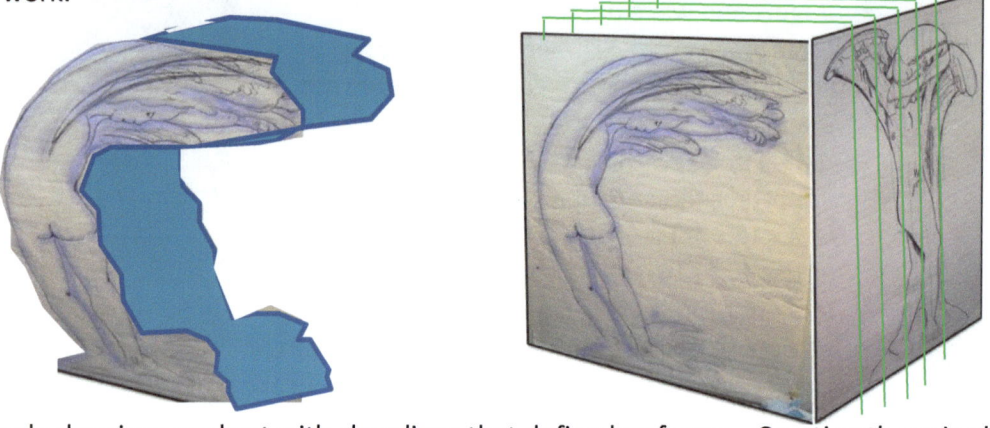

Direct, simple drawings are best with clear lines that define key forms. Creating these is all about proportion and position. If you had mechanical drawing you have a clue. Your maquette and your eye position will have to give you the clues to get it created. Tape up your two pieces of paper side by side and mark the maximum height and base line (floor). If you're starting in PowerPoint you can position your photos side by side and place some horizontal lines to key elements. Had I known this on this project I would have shot picks more carefully and avoided the reconciliation work on the drawing. (Note how my details don't align well here).

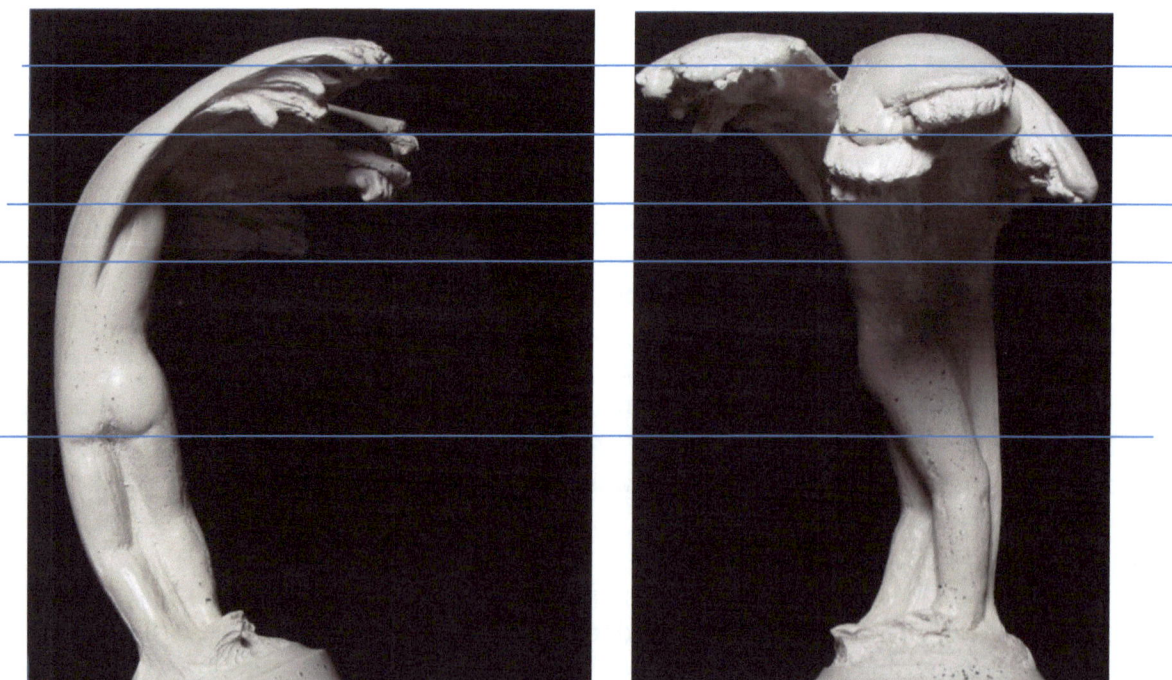

Enlargement from a Maquette
Creating Control Drawing Views with the Projector

We've done our best to get our picks. We've cajoled some gear to make our magic lantern show. Our paper is up on the wall with some lines to help us get the dimensions.   So we project.

Once the lamp is on, draw your lines in pencil. You will make them heavier with marker later after everything checks out. If you can do this in the studio it is easier, just move the projector for view 2*.*
You will need about 12 feet of projection distance for a 6 foot high image. **Layouts are not works of art. They are tools we will use again and again to facilitate construction of the form. Good defined lines and accurate ability to measure are more important than beauty.**

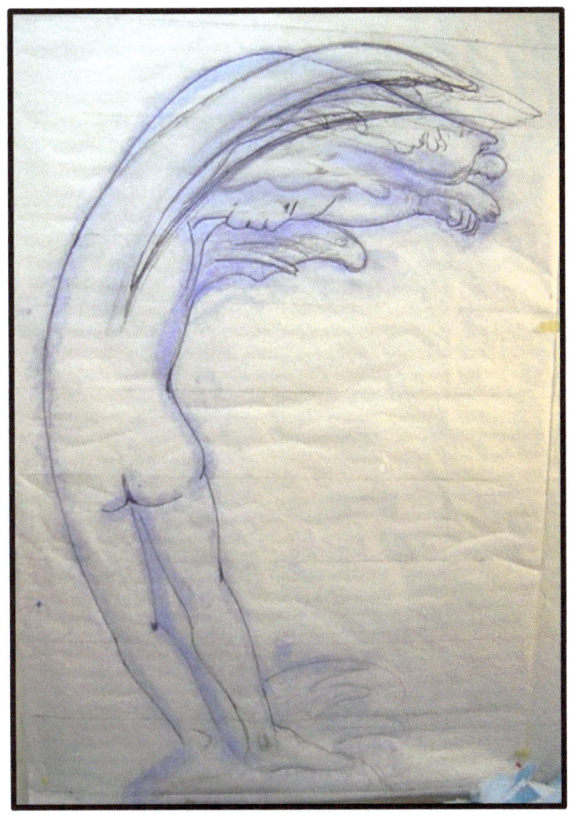

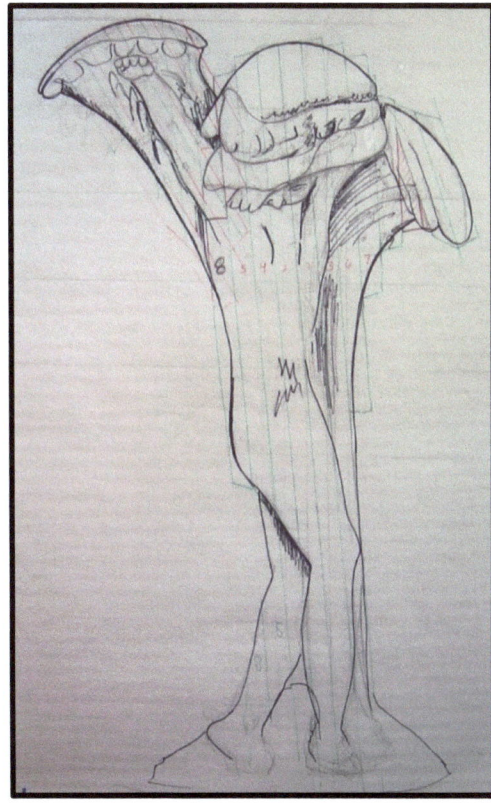

Note: I didn't get any photos while projecting. See page 39.

These drawings were shot after use. The lines are darkened and bold. The blue is from the pounce process, not for beauty, but I like it.

Side View

End View

Our maquette has been studied prior to this event and is, as always, nearby to reference from. (Note the pencil lines). This one got knocked over several times and wound up all taped together

The projector is a great tool for going large. Here is a shot of a study with all the figures from this installation.

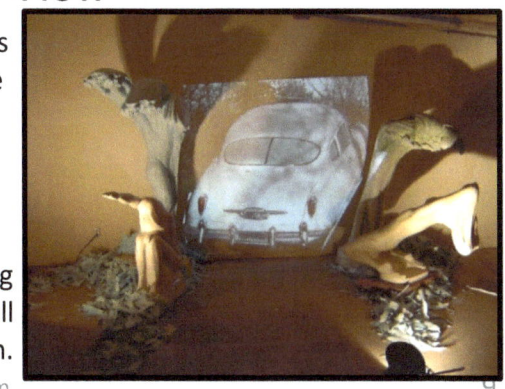

Creating the Layout Drawing

You want to use a reasonably stout paper, wide enough to capture your entire side view. Butcher paper will do and you can tape it together if it is not wide enough. Here is where you determine just how high and wide the work will be. You will need to take the paper on and off the wall many times so don't tape it permanently. Leave enough margin for working, pinning and tape tears. I use push pins. It helps to put a few horizontal lines across both pieces for referencing the projected image and the two pieces to each other. Your height and base are good lines to have and maybe a few even increments in between.

You sketch over the projected image in pencil so you can make changes. Once you have the major lines and forms on the paper and have wrung out all information possible from the projected images, you can shut off the projector. The two views should be side by side at the same height, with major features at the same elevation in both views. Features not visible behind other forms should be drawn in if you can, maybe in another color or line style.

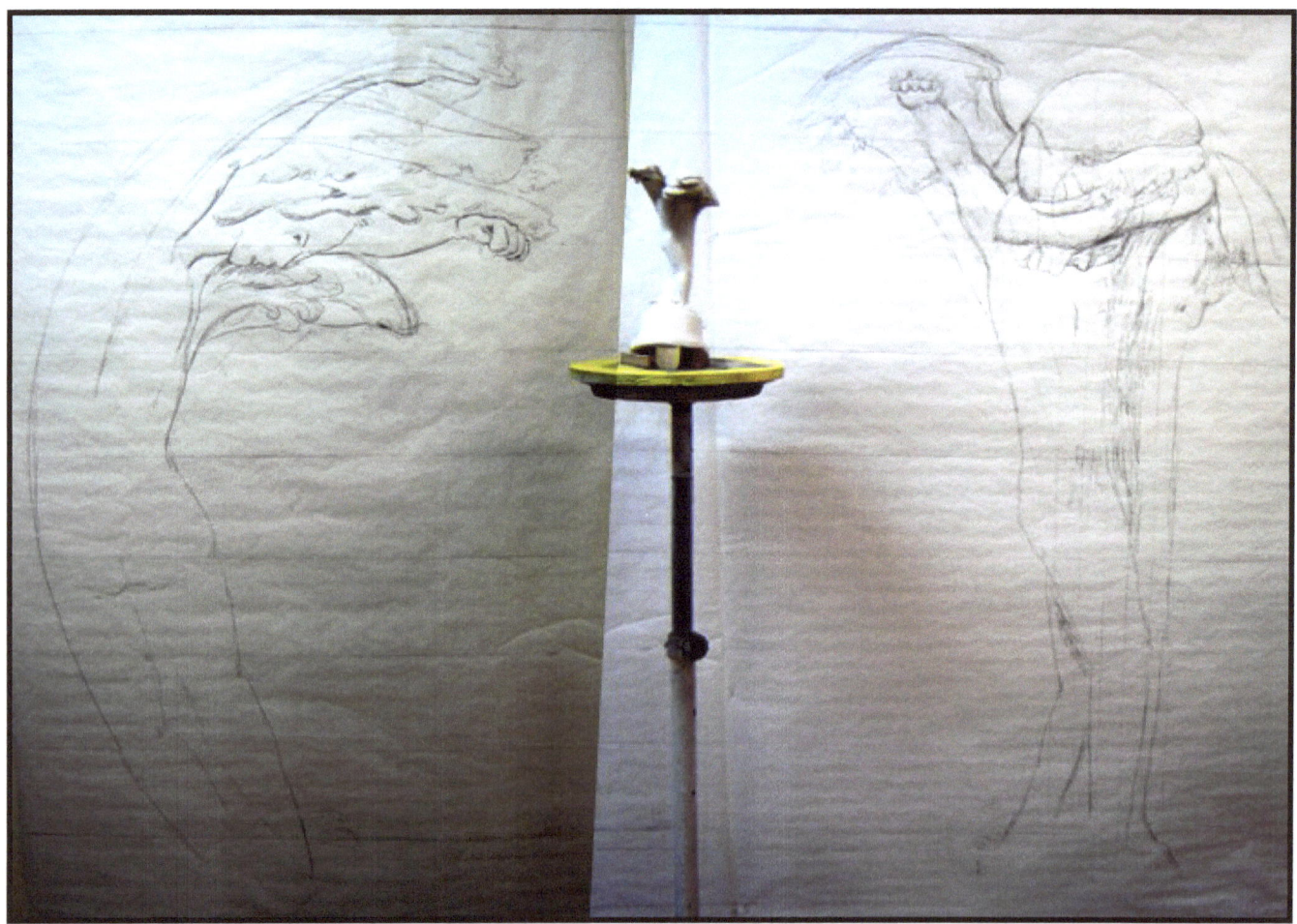

Before you darken the lines, step back and seriously think about what is important to building the piece. You want to define the edges of separate forms and appendages and be able to block these in from the information on these two views. It is very important that the forms are accurately conveyed in both views, and that the dimensions match. Often photography and projection distort things so you need to check it all out. Compare the maquette and make sure you are happy with proportion and position of everything.

Reconciling Your Layout

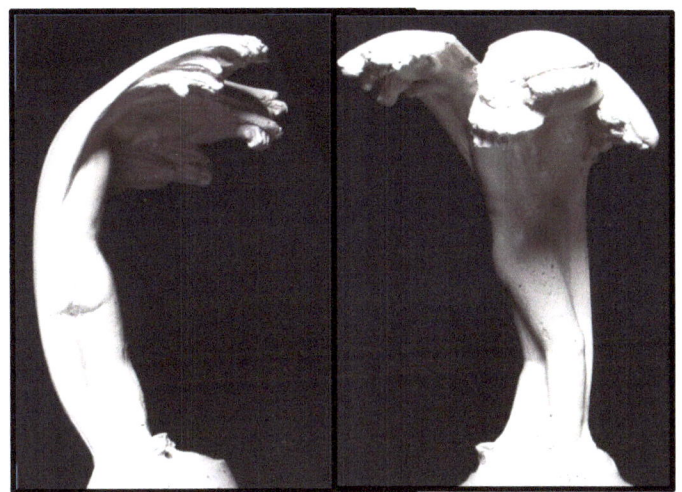

Getting these two drawings dimensionally reconciled is crucial to the project. You lay out a few horizontal lines as guides across both views. This is quickly done by using a level as a straight edge. I drop down vertically at regular dimension intervals. Here it was 200 millimeters (about 8").

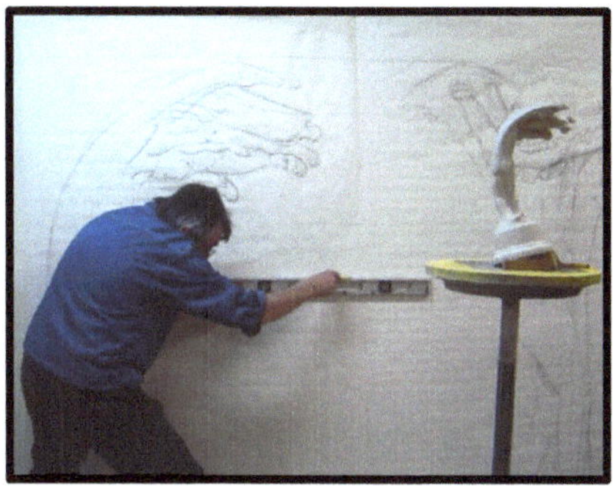

Next, identify major features in both views and check distances from your guidelines with a scale, ruler, compass or calipers. If they don't match, adjust your drawing until they do. Here you can see that my initial drawings were OK at the hands and face but did not match well at the cheek of the butt. I altered the drawing to move the end view feature down to match the side view. This is a result of slightly different camera angles when I shot the maquette. Now you are ready to sweeten up your lines and make key lines bolder with a marker. Since your templating will come from the side view we focus on these lines the most.

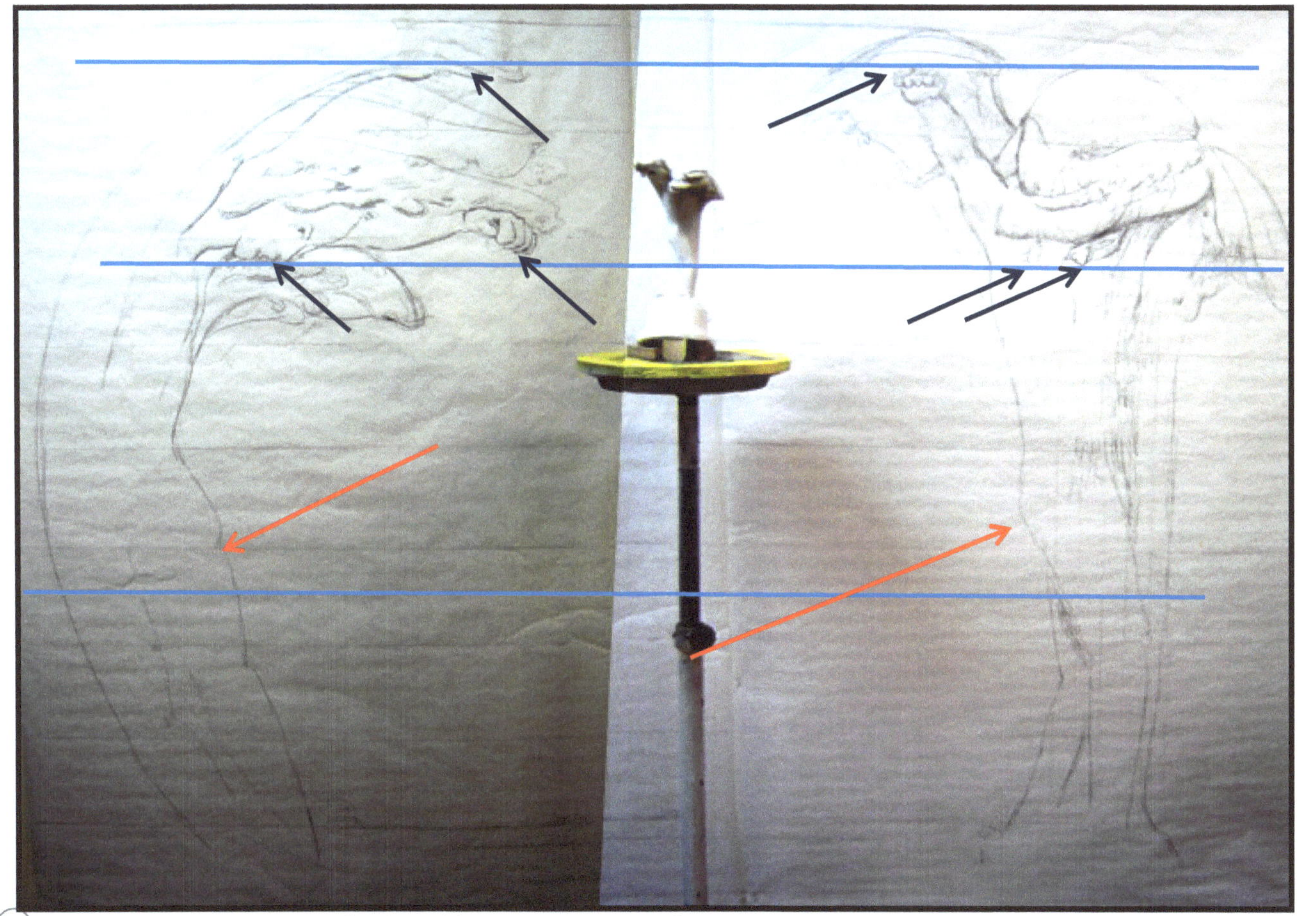

Calculating the Stack Up of Planks (Sections)

To figure out the placement and number of foam panels to cut, you start by selecting an axis in the end view. Place a foam board up against the drawing and draw a line on either side. (A different color for these helps reduce confusion). Check where features on the piece wind up along the board and adjust to your advantage. Here the laminations are just off vertical to let us get the entire forward leg and the centerline of the face into one plank. Continue tracing out plank thicknesses to see how many pieces you will need and what size they are.   At this stage you are constantly checking from view to view to consider seam lines. Consider putting lines on the maquette to help visualize where the seams wind up. You do not want a seam across a skinny appendage causing a weak joint. A seam leaving a thin piece of foam on a diagonal across a crowned surface later shows up as a broad swatch of glue, or weak piece when you carve.

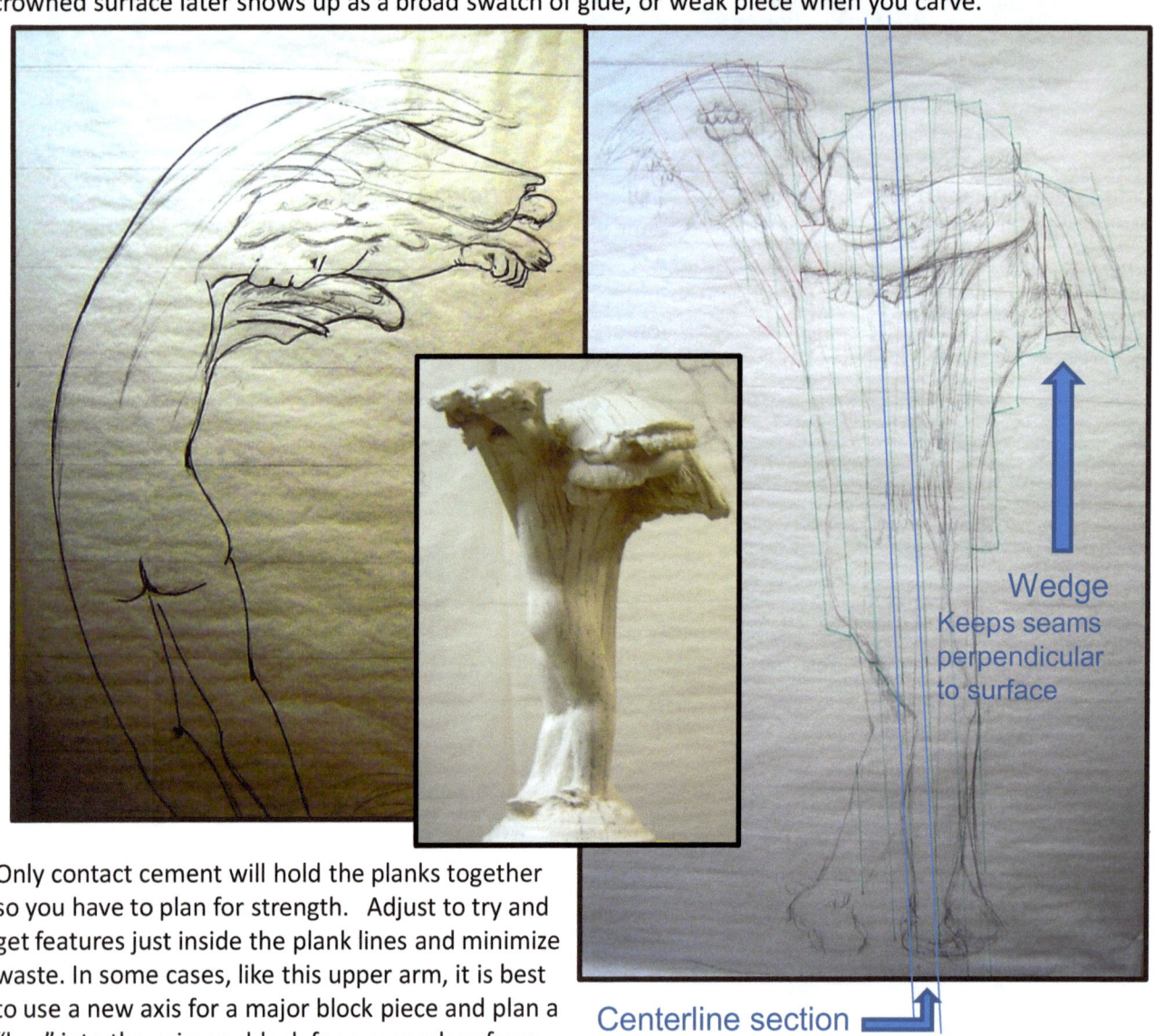

Wedge
Keeps seams perpendicular to surface

Centerline section

Only contact cement will hold the planks together so you have to plan for strength. Adjust to try and get features just inside the plank lines and minimize waste. In some cases, like this upper arm, it is best to use a new axis for a major block piece and plan a "key" into the primary block for a secondary form.

Also you can see that a slight wedge was placed in under the side wing at the far left. This allows carving the majority of that surface from one plank. These two views now allow building the block from sheets of foam. We know the shape to cut from the side view and the length and placement of each plank from the end view. We are ready to begin cutting foam.

Major Blocks
to Construct

Now the consideration is:
In what order to build pieces?

Blocks for carving need to be laminated
from the 2" planks and then glued or keyed
together. You now need to decide how to
create them and what order of construction
will best facilitate this build.
I chose four major blocks, and a few "add
ons" at the base and along the arch of #2.
Only the area here in red under #3 could
not be cut directly from 2" plank.

The joint between #2 and #1 blocks would
be difficult to get good alignment. The
construction is important due to the weight
of the appendage and length of the arching
piece that hangs on this joint. (This later
proved problematic. See the last page
addition on this topic)

Obviously block #1 is the main item to start
on. How soon to add others depends on the
process you invent to stabilize this thing
while you carve. #4 was added early to
allow it to stand. #3 was constructed but not
attached immediately to allow it to rest on
this side on the bench while you hog off
material on the major sections. Details on
the base area were not filled in until much
later. The simple flat planks in the base area
allowed clamping the block down for
aggressive work.

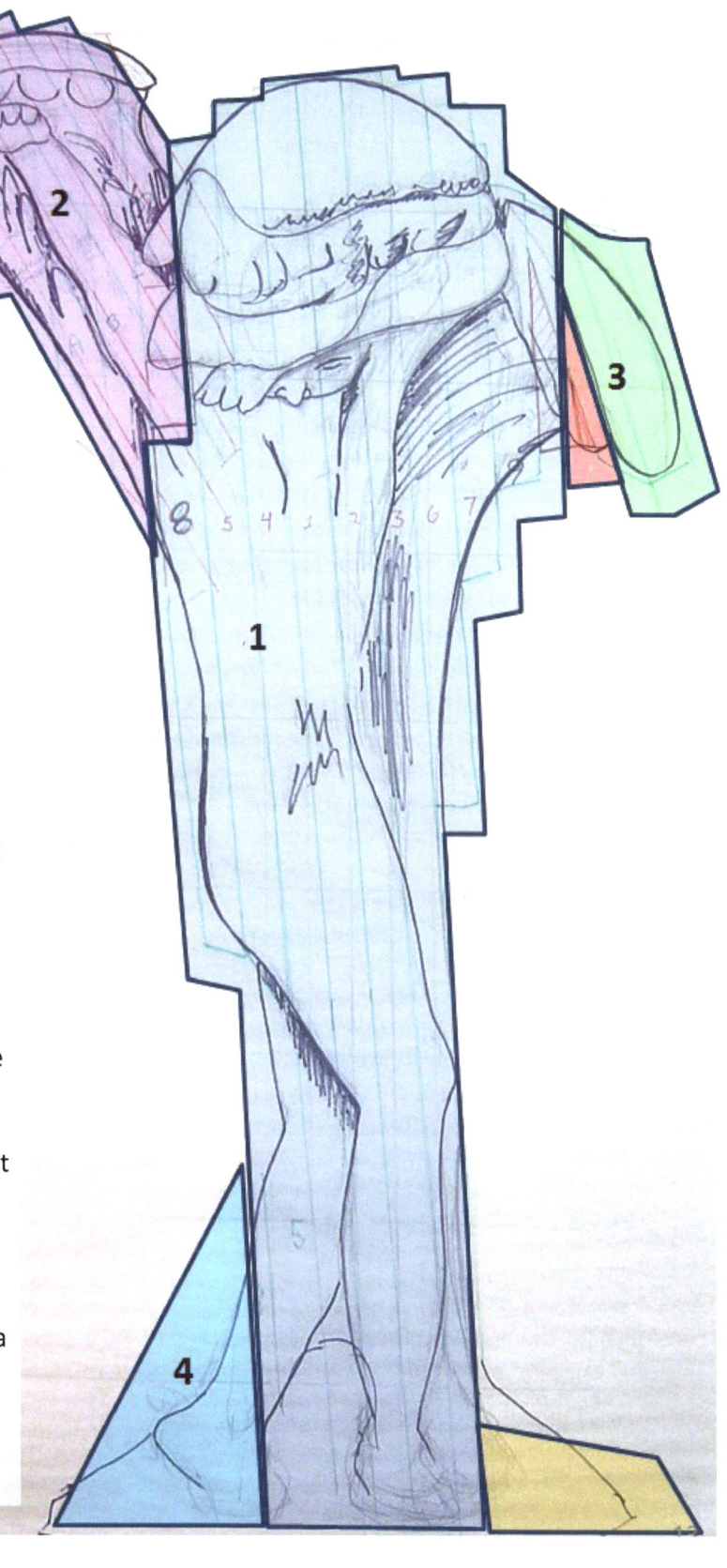

About Foam - Types, Nature and Applications

There are two common types: **Polyurethane**, and **Polystyrene**. Urethanes are impervious to solvents and can be used with any type of resins, paints and finishing materials (polyester boat resins and bondo for example). Styrene is way more sensitive to solvents and you can't go near it with acetone, lacquer thinner, polyester resin, or many other solvents. It will dissolve. (I have a funny story about this from Italy, but that's for another day). This is why you must be careful with glue. Incredibly, epoxy resins and alcohol (which dissolves unhardened epoxy and shellac) are fine to use with styrene. Urethane foam is generally yellow. You can buy urethane as a 2 part liquid which, when mixed together, foam up several times the volume of liquid and then sets and becomes rigid. It can be purchased in sheet and block but is expensive. This document will not cover urethanes.   There are also **open cell, closed cell** and **bead board** types of foam, which will not be covered completely here.

Styrene bead is the cheaper stuff that you recognize from coffee cups and those cheap coolers you see in pieces along the road and washing up at the beach. These items are fragile and easily trashed. Bead board is made by expanding styrene beads with steam in a closed chamber or mold where they stick together. Mass produced Items are done like this. Floatation and construction materials are produced in huge chambers. If there is a company like this near by, you might consider getting thick blocks to work with. But the quality can be difficult. Bead board with greater density can carve fairly well but it is hard to find. Most of the bead board at the hardware store is crumbly and only suitable for insulation.

Extruded styrene foam is much tougher, has virtually no voids and carves beautifully. This stuff has a small closed cell that is not crumbly and holds a shape very well. It can be sanded to a very nice surface quickly and is readily available at building material outlets. It is usually pink or blue, and not the common white of bead board. It comes in ½ to 2" thicknesses and can be purchased in some areas in thicker billet blocks for dock floatation.

Gluing Styrene Foam

Styrene can be stuck to itself and other materials with contact cements that do not have solvents that attack it. (**Always test** before trying anything new). 3M Spray 77 is my choice. It will dissolve styrene if applied too thick, but if sprayed in a nice even thin coat to both surfaces and allowed to tack up it will stick them together very well. The bite makes the bond pretty permanent. You can use 5 minute epoxy as well but any hard material like this in a glue joint will make carving a nightmare. You cannot get a good surface across a glue joint unless the glue is about the same hardness as the foam. 3M spray 78 is made for foam and will not dissolve it. This and 3M spray 90 however have a bigger nozzle orifice and come out in greater quantity. You will use more glue and not get any better adhesion with either. I have tried a few other types but the 77 seems to work best and most consistently.

Perfect fit, even thorough spray coverage and tack time are important to a solid joint. Fit your pieces carefully. (I put little tick marks across the joint to aid in alignment). Clean off all crumbs, you don't want anything but glue in the joint. Spray both pieces, let the glue tack up. (When it is not liquid, but still sticky). Then align and squeeze them together and pound the materials to squash out the air and distribute the glue. Sometimes clamping is helpful. Once a broad amount of surface has contacted there is little chance for adjustment, so placement is tricky, but a little practice and some markings will make it easy. The set is instant and you can go immediately to the next piece. You will not be able to pull most joints apart without tearing foam. You will get small gaps. (Not to worry. There are techniques for dealing with this).

Ready to Cut Material

Making some marks on the maquette will also help you see the new construction and plan the build. You are constantly reviewing both the maquette and the layout to plan.

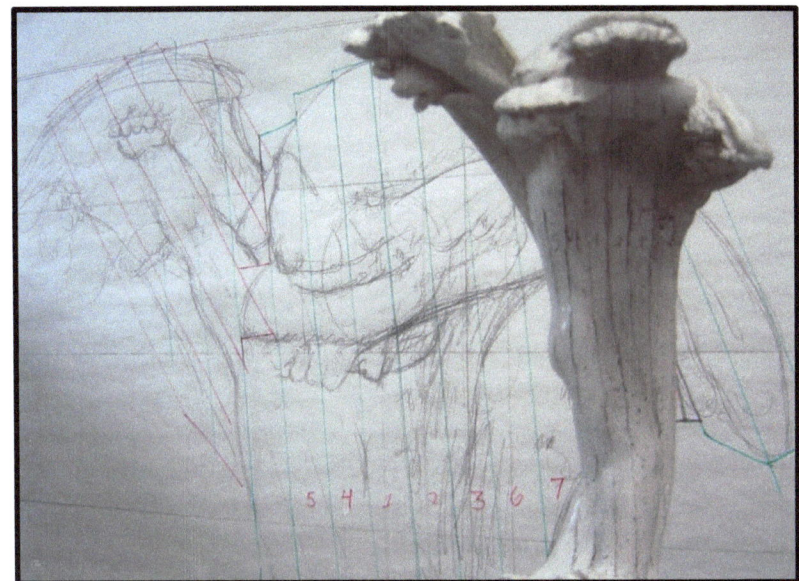

It is a good idea to label the sections. You will be cutting a lot of planks and pieces that look very similar and may not get glued up in the order that they are drawn or cut.

We numbered them in the order of cutting and assembly. The coinciding numbers on the maquette help you see the job and adjust for potential problems.

Positioning the First Piece

The first piece you cut out will be the guide to all the rest. You want a section close to the center line and you want to plan a base that will allow this model to stand on its own and support it's own weight. This key section will have lines on it that indicate where other pieces locate. Now you take the side view off the wall and place it on the sheet of foam. Position it for best conservation of material. If there is a tight fit to get multiple pieces cut from the sheet, you may want to try a few positions and measure to get the most from each sheet. Pin it with push pins so it can't slide around. You need a good scale to draw the base line.

On this job we could get two centerline sections from the sheet by reversing one and pushing all the way to the corner.

Caution: In Foam sheet manufactured with score lines, (for easy breaking), you need to be aware of how these might effect the strength of the work.

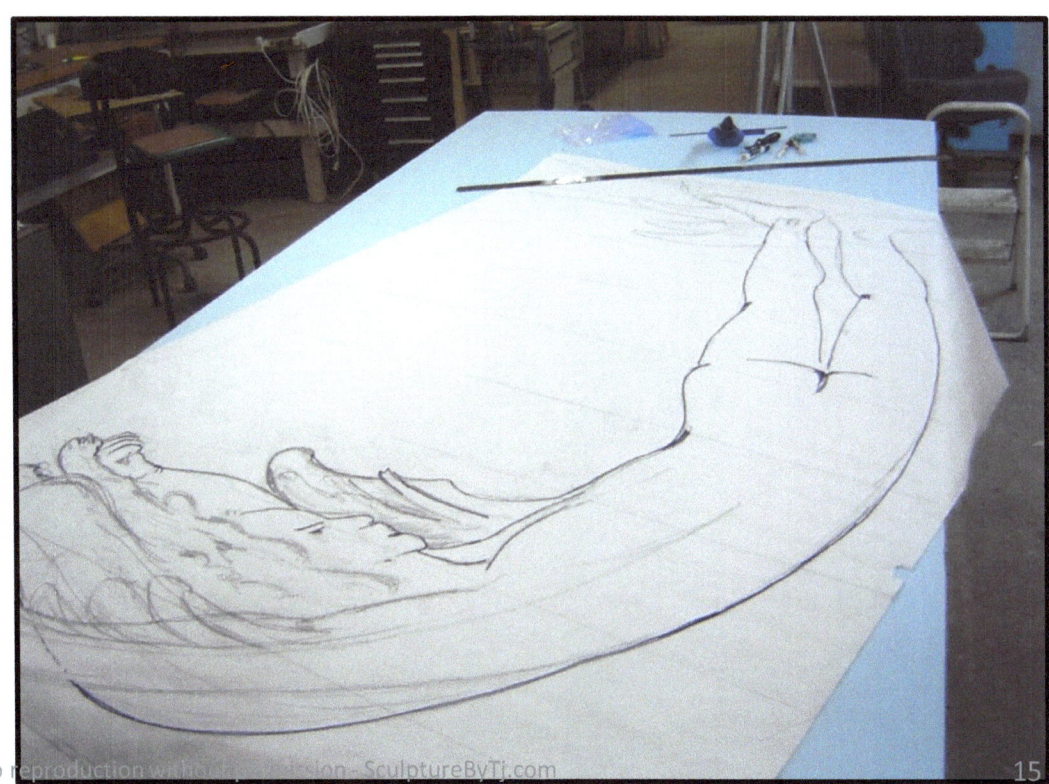

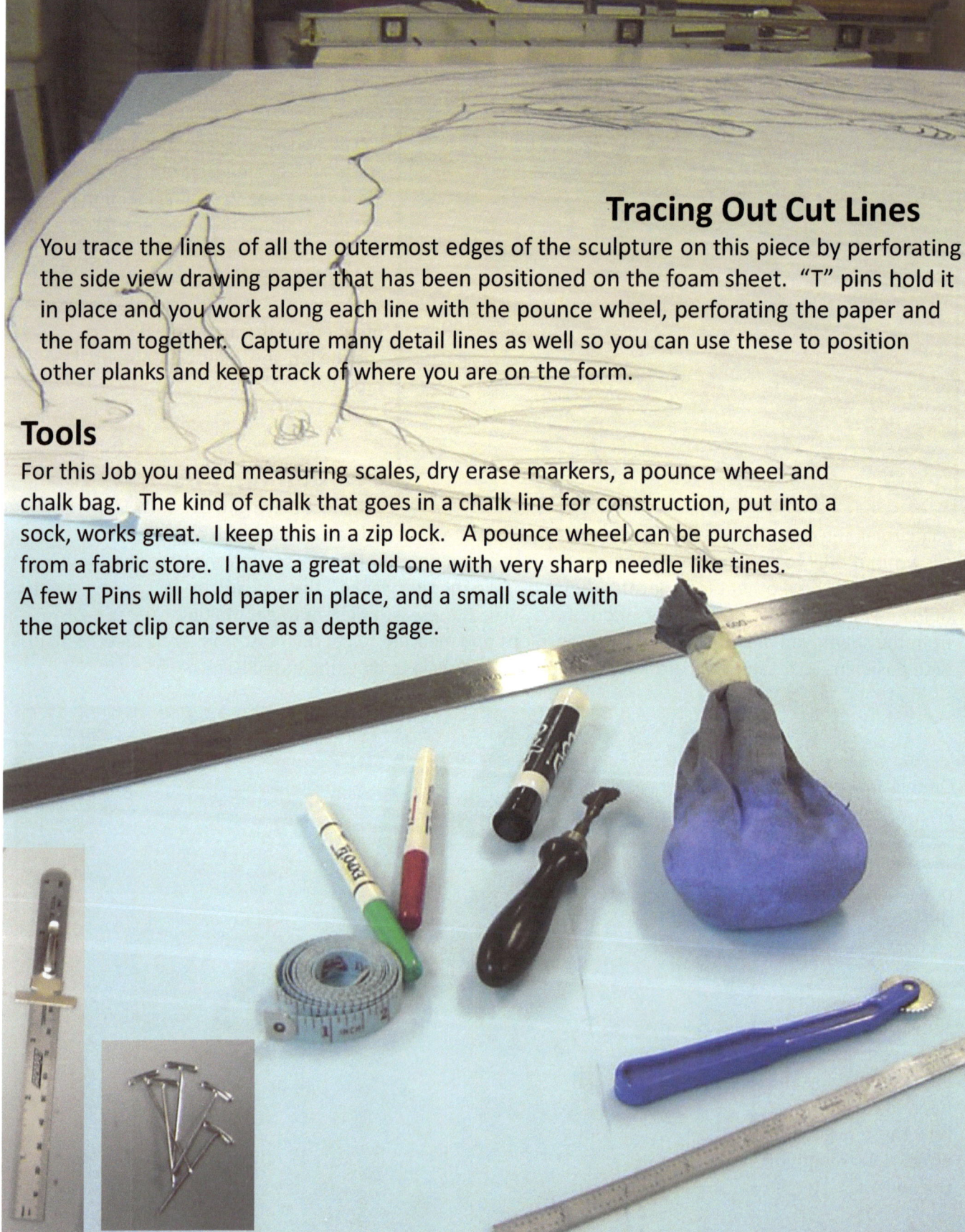

Tracing Out Cut Lines

You trace the lines of all the outermost edges of the sculpture on this piece by perforating the side view drawing paper that has been positioned on the foam sheet. "T" pins hold it in place and you work along each line with the pounce wheel, perforating the paper and the foam together. Capture many detail lines as well so you can use these to position other planks and keep track of where you are on the form.

Tools

For this Job you need measuring scales, dry erase markers, a pounce wheel and chalk bag. The kind of chalk that goes in a chalk line for construction, put into a sock, works great. I keep this in a zip lock. A pounce wheel can be purchased from a fabric store. I have a great old one with very sharp needle like tines. A few T Pins will hold paper in place, and a small scale with the pocket clip can serve as a depth gage.

Transferring Lines

Trace out lines and pounce them with the chalk bag. This pushes the chalk through the holes and marks the foam so you can see them. Once the paper template has holes you can position it on another sheet and just pounce it again with chalk to make another one.

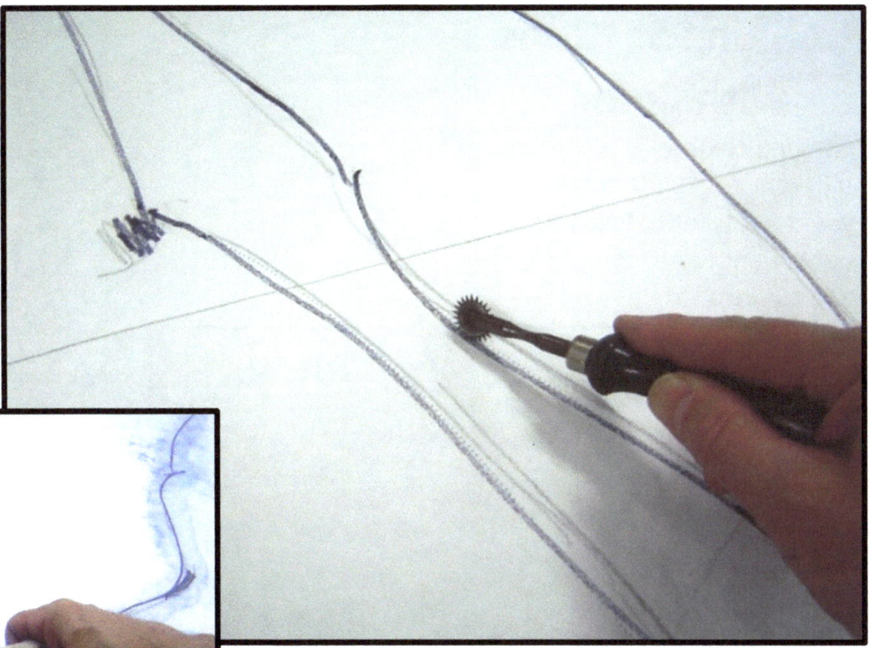

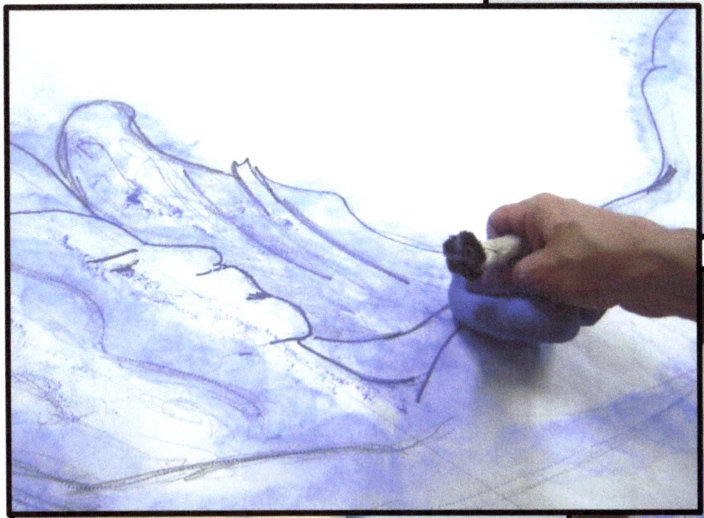

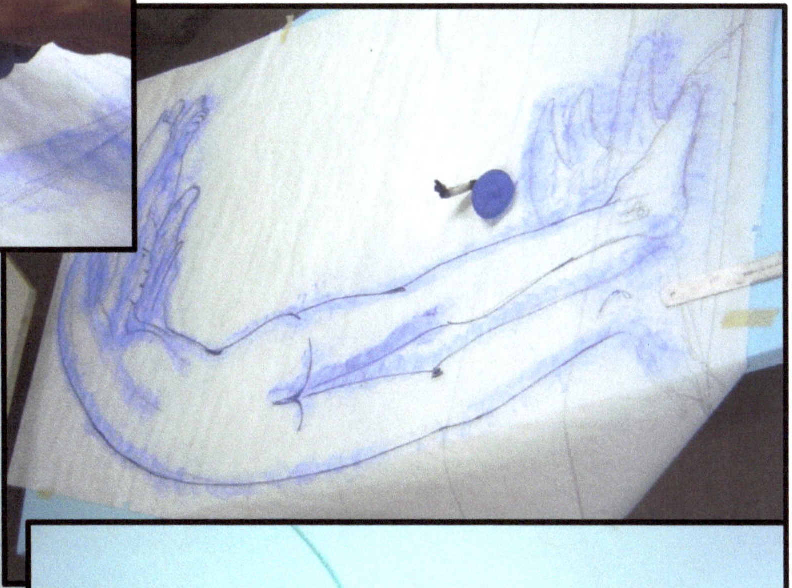

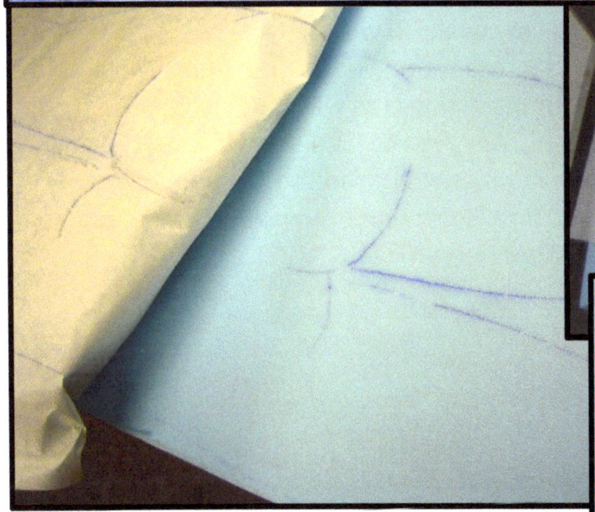

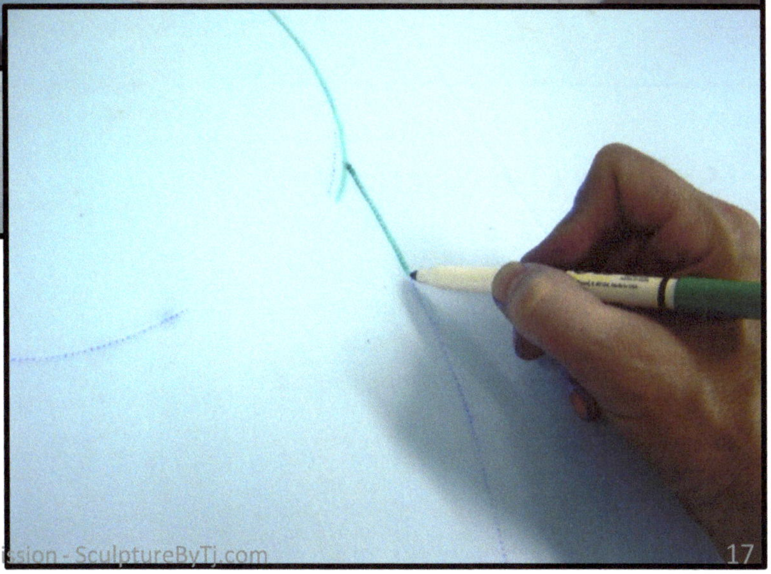

When the paper is peeled back the line is visible but a little weak. Trace over with dry erase to make sure you can read it while you are cutting. Dry erase marker will not dissolve foam where others will.

Defining Sections with Color

Use one color for cut lines and different colors for details that you don't want to lose but don't want to get confused and cut into either.

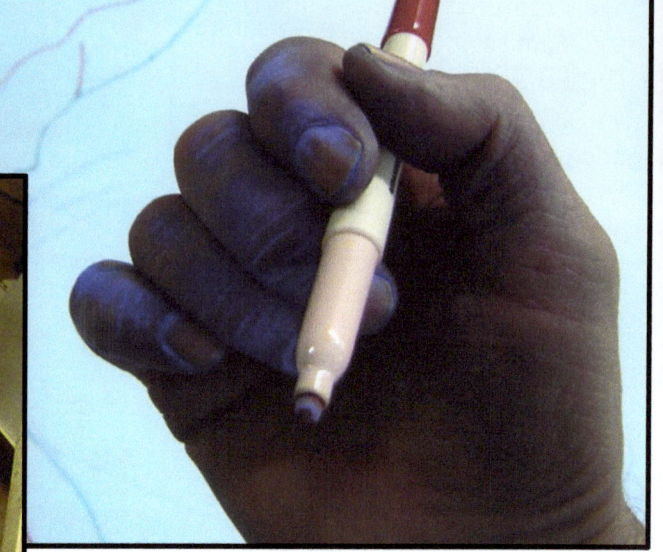

Cutting Tools

A band saw can be very helpful and I use mine constantly in this process. But it is limited by the depth of throat. Trying to balance an 8 foot sheet and push it through the saw while staying on the lines is very tricky. Many cuts are not possible. Most of your beginning cuts will have to be done by hand. Any type of hole saw will do. The key is a stout enough blade to not bend while you stroke through the material at a reach.

Sawing Out Sections

Stay well outside your lines to help compensate for a cut that is less than perfectly vertical. You want a little extra material to give you more options when you are carving the surface.

Cutting Sections

Most the work is keeping the tool vertical.   Any toothed blade will cut this stuff easily. You just saw away until the pieces can be separated.

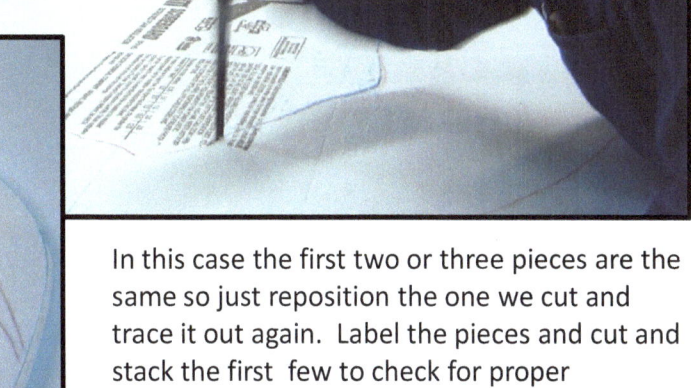

In this case the first two or three pieces are the same so just reposition the one we cut and trace it out again. Label the pieces and cut and stack the first few to check for proper alignment and consider how you will create a base that allows the piece to stand.

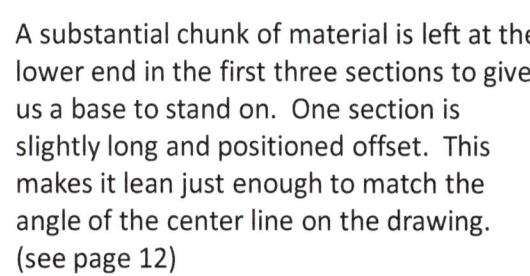

A substantial chunk of material is left at the lower end in the first three sections to give us a base to stand on. One section is slightly long and positioned offset. This makes it lean just enough to match the angle of the center line on the drawing. (see page 12)

Glue Laminating

Once you are sure of positioning you spray both pieces with 3M 77 spray adhesive. Allow the glue a few moments to tack up. The pieces are carefully positioned and set. Then pound hard with an open hand to squeeze them together.

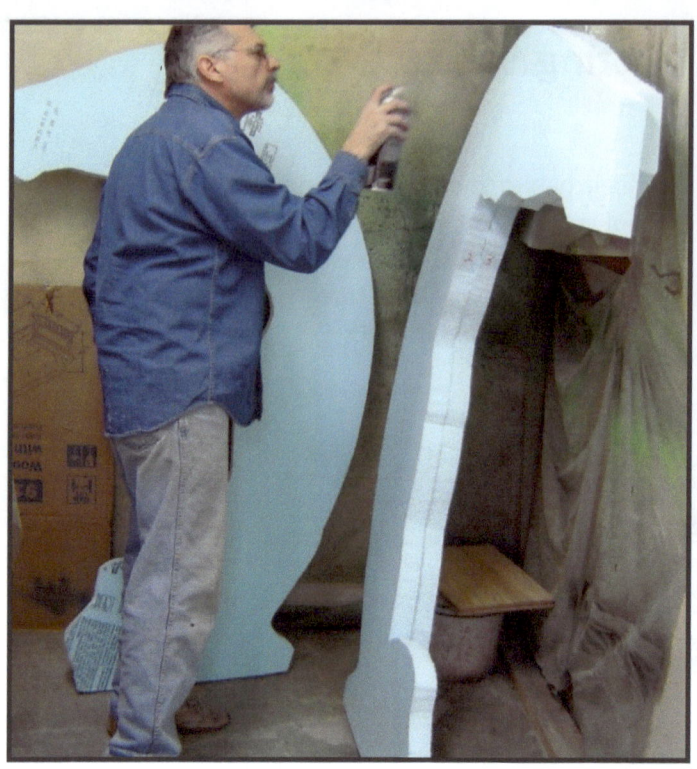

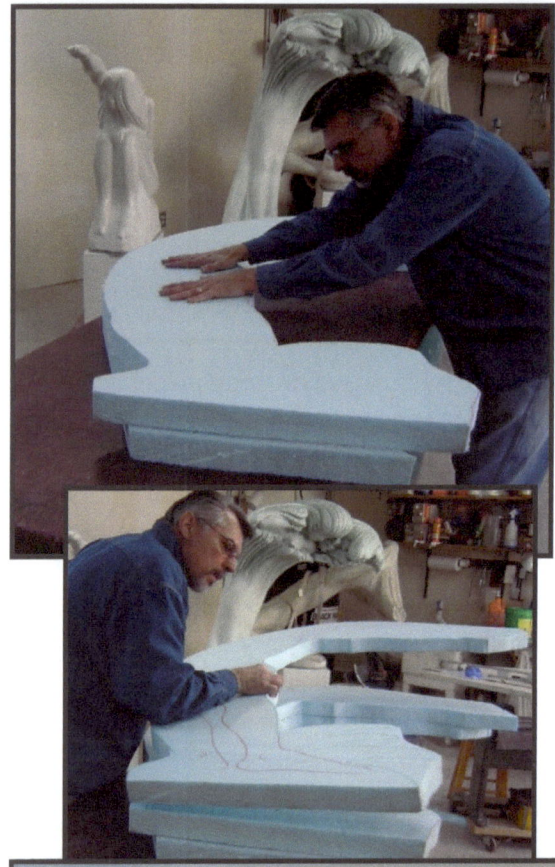

It is a good idea to trial fit, trace edges and add locating marks to help you place them just right. Once they stick there is no going back without some tearing of material, so you have to get it right the first time. Some plastic on the walls and on surfaces in the spray area is a good idea if you are going to do much of this. You keep assembling until it will stand, and you can compare to the drawings. I've tried several adhesives. Spray 77 works the best and you get more coverage from a can than with the "foam specific" 78 due to nozzle design.

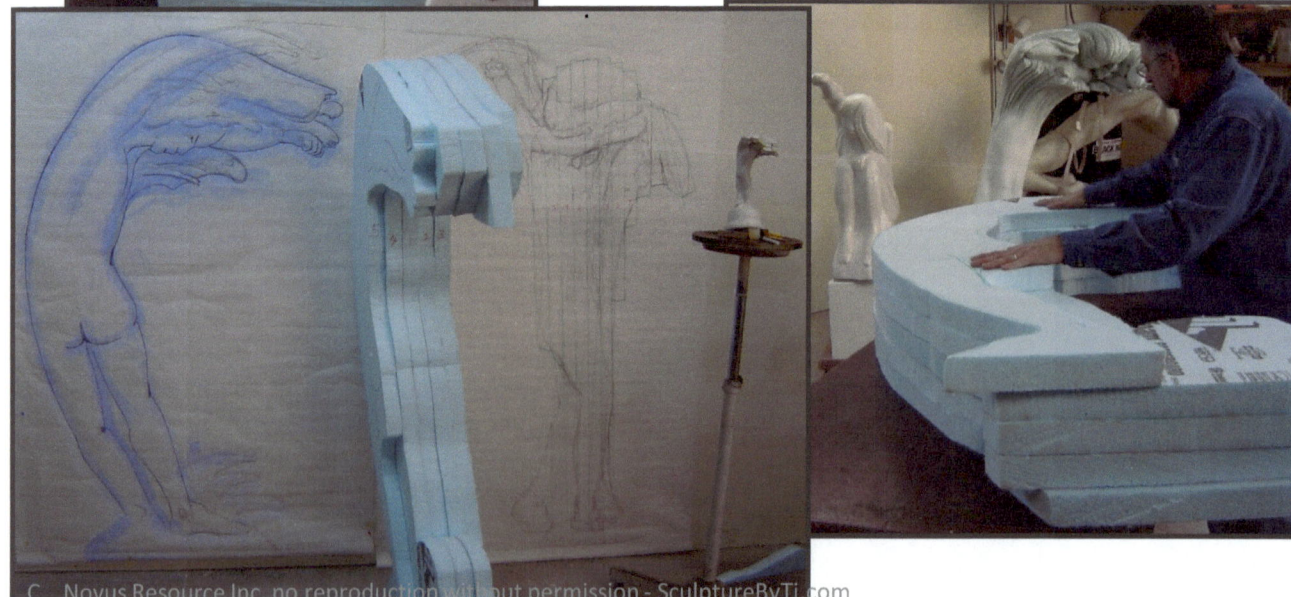

Adding a Support

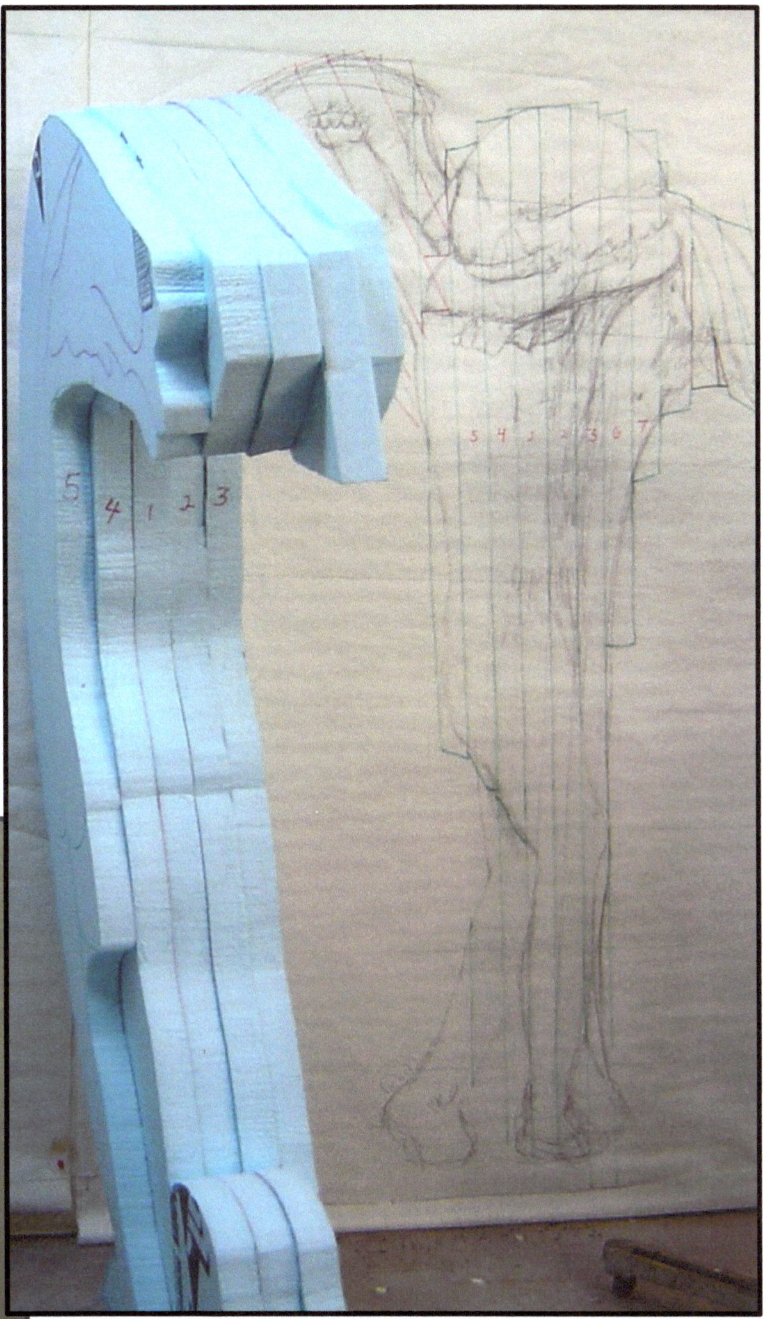

Here are all the large center sections have been stack laminated. Note that the forward leg needs no material past section 4, so section 5 has been cut back to the line of the rear leg in that area.

 #5 is the last one that goes all the way to the floor from the top. Pieces to the left of this will depend on the joinery for strength. Those that carry weight will need to be keyed in for strength.

The lower leg protrusion will only be attached at the calf. This is too small a surface area for a strong joint and could be a potential break with the weight and abuse of supporting the whole form. The form needs material jutting out at a 90 degree angle to give it support and stability. This appendage will create a base and carry the weight from above.

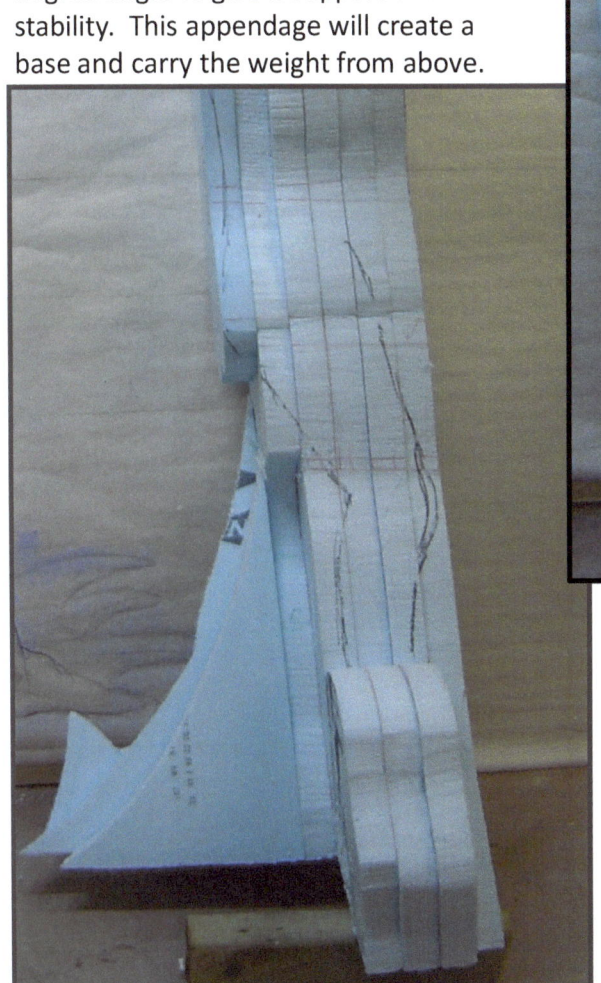

For strength you must introduce a key way to make the attachment solid and able to bear the weight and impacts it will get without fracturing.

It is a good idea to leave some pieces protruding at 90 degree angles down here where we will finish last. The base area takes a lot of abuse and we use it to fixture the work and hold it fast while we carve more delicate areas above. (see later picks on page 28)

Adding a Support

You measure how much is needed on the drawing and cut some pieces to join in at a right angle to this leg. The strength of a buttress is achieved by notching in the center piece. It is made long and cut with a protruding key . In this instance it doesn't need much, 3/4 inch will do if it's tight. The area to be notched has been drawn on section 5. You cut down in strips to your depth with a marked blade or depth cutting tool.

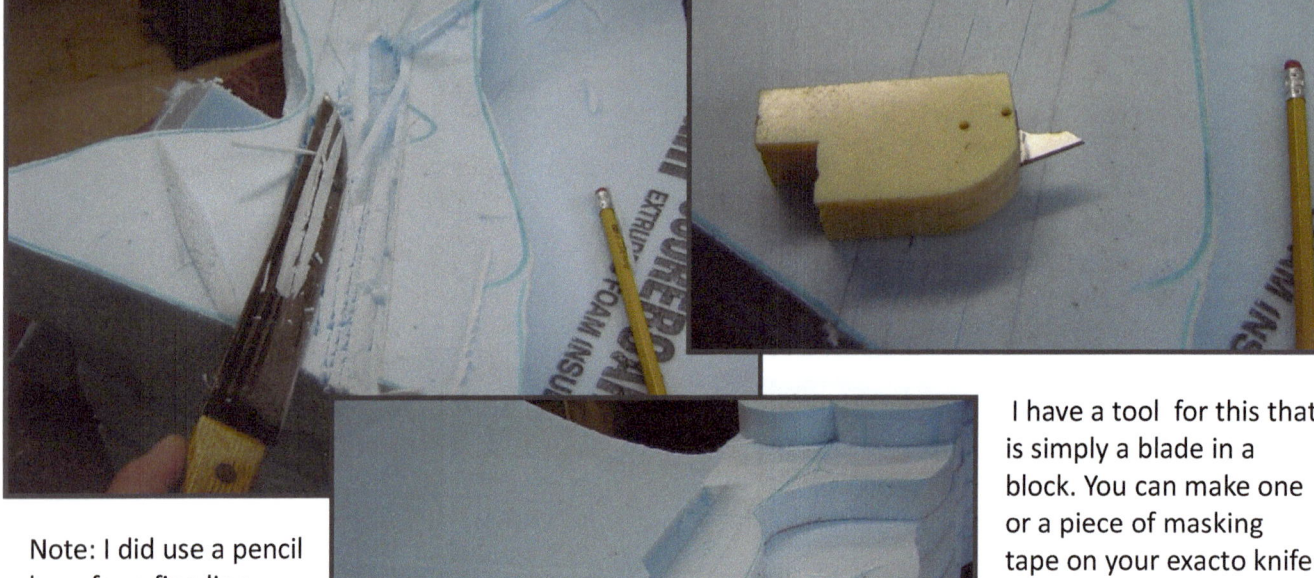

Note: I did use a pencil here for a fine line. Joinery requires a bit more accuracy.

I have a tool for this that is simply a blade in a block. You can make one or a piece of masking tape on your exacto knife will do this job also. Just keep it vertical on the cuts along the lines. You cut down to the depth, make some V cuts and start removing strips of material. When you can get in with a larger blade you lay it sideways and take out the rest.

The buttress piece is cut with a small tongue and fitted to the notch. You want it tight, so stay inside your lines. When it all fits well you spray glue in the notch and on the tongue and assemble them. Now the pieces on either side can be added and the whole joint will be strong.

Keyed in Appendage

Now to deal with the big arm form that juts from the body at an angle. The red lines on the drawing are the second guess at where to put the seams. It was evident that this would need extra attention at the joint, so we started by designing a step at the top of plank 8 which would be matched by the block form. The planks of new block (red lines) were cut and assembled one at a time to get the angle trimmed just right. This group was labeled *A,B,C,D,E*. The key thing here is knowing we have enough material in this block to get the whole form. In the side view the lines are being viewed at an angle which means they are foreshortened slightly. The solution to this is to measure the overall height of the plank in the end view and use that dimension for cutting out planks. I also left the cuts full from my lines and did them one at a time to put them on the job and look at the results.

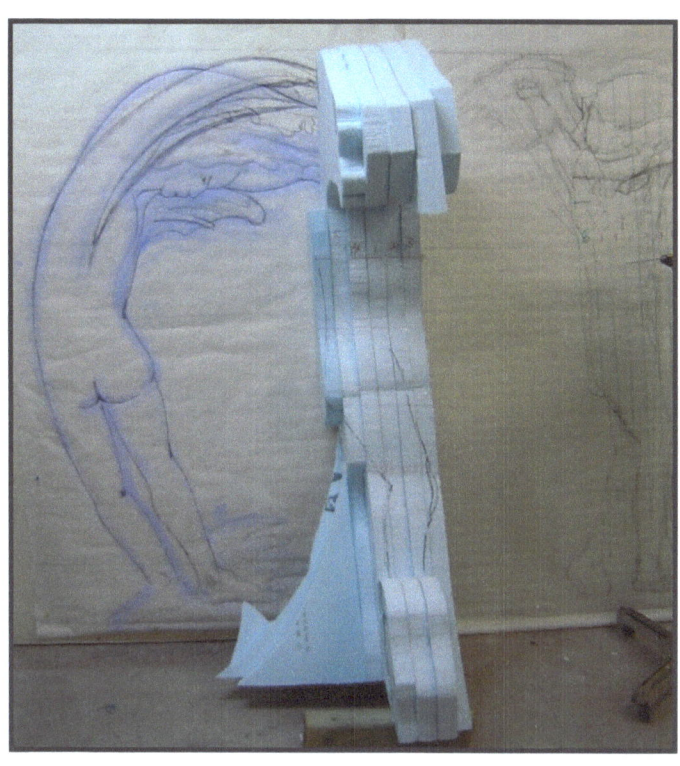

Section "B" sits on top of plank 8. The side view arc for this piece must come from the dimension measured here, not exactly what we see in the foreshortened side view. Alter the ark to match the dimensions after tracing the pattern for this arm on the plank. (It grows slightly).

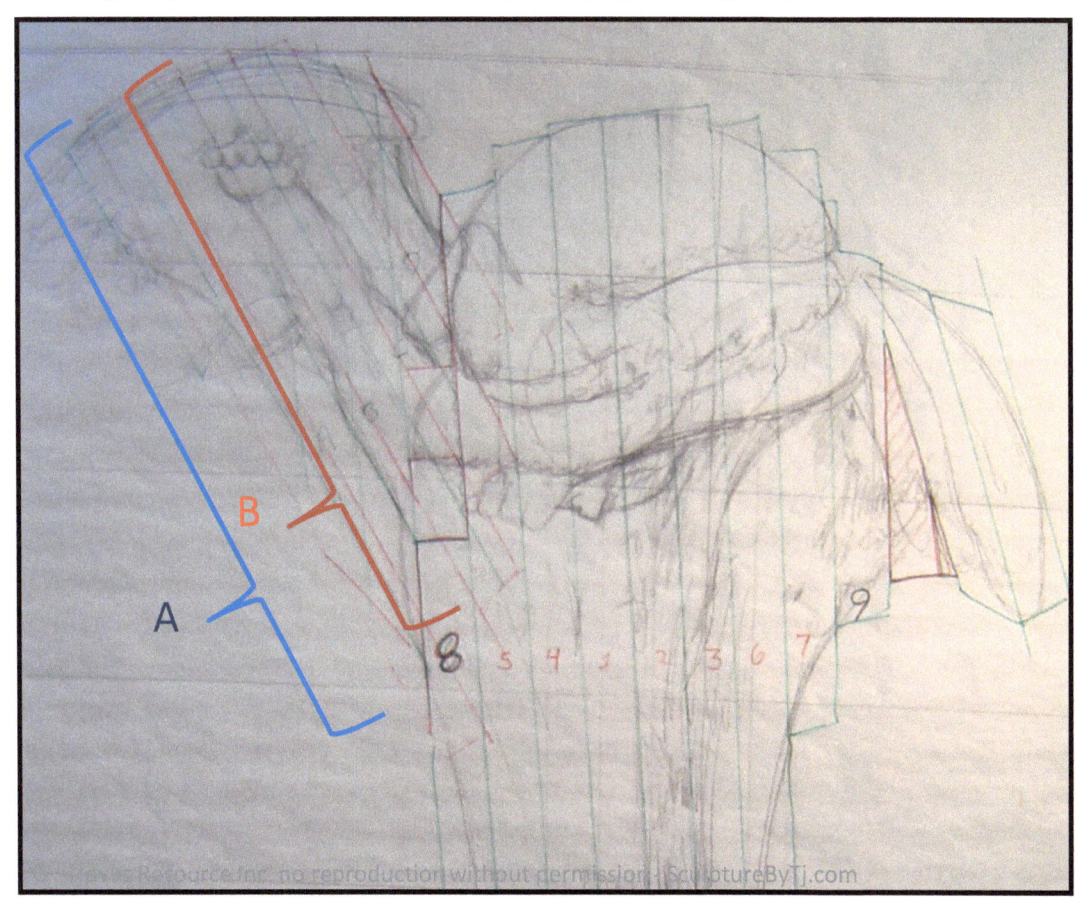

Remember the length of each plank has to include the material needed to get the angle cut. The lines on the drawing (red) extend out through the other form, (plank 5) adding to the rough cut length.

Keyed in Appendage

To get the line from the side view you can used the old "piece of plastic" trick. Pin a sheet of plastic over the drawing and trace the line you want with marker. The first thing is to measure the arc using the height of the end of plank 8 as a reference and make sure you have enough stock to get what we need when attached at an angle. (previous page).

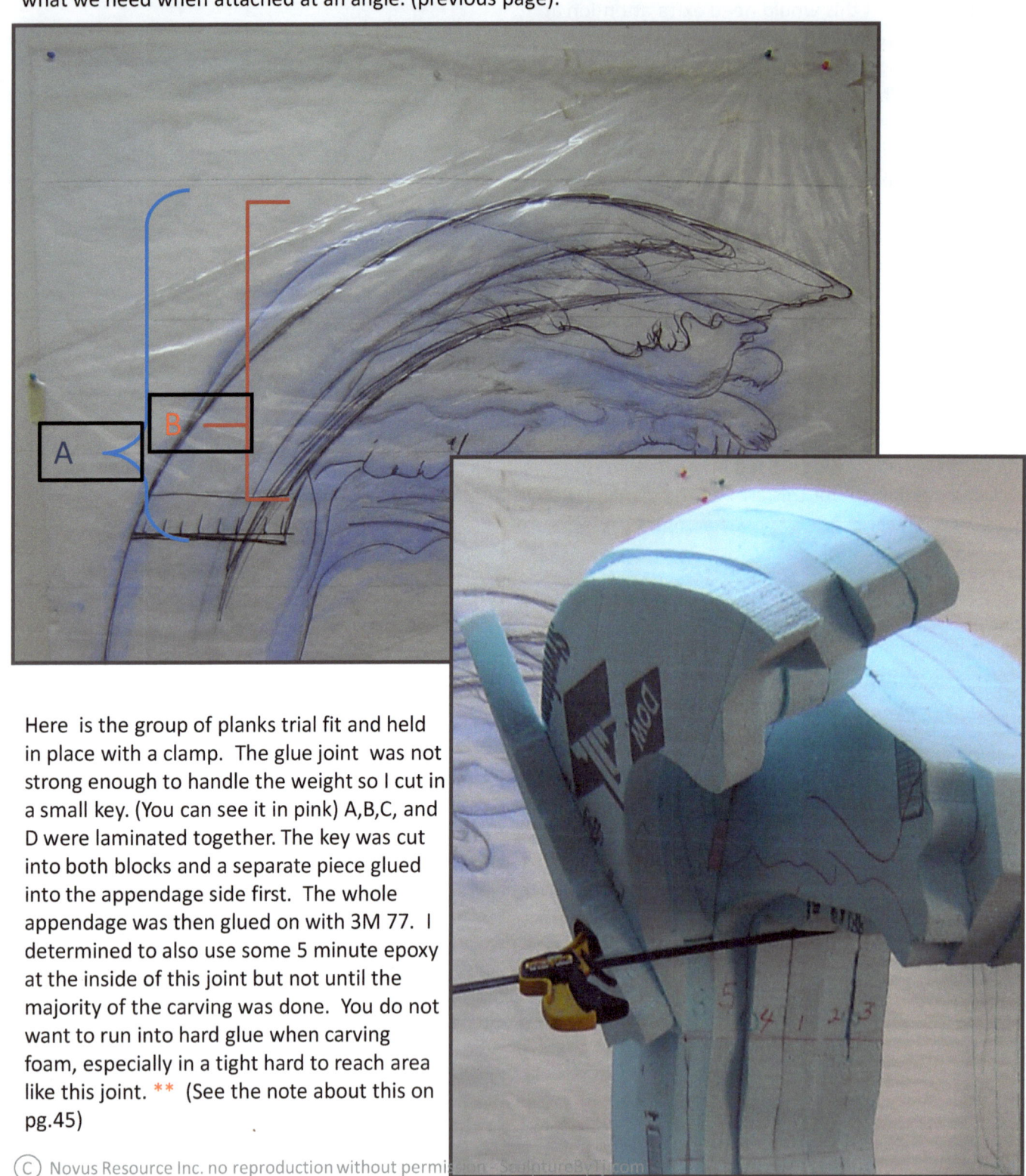

Here is the group of planks trial fit and held in place with a clamp. The glue joint was not strong enough to handle the weight so I cut in a small key. (You can see it in pink) A,B,C, and D were laminated together. The key was cut into both blocks and a separate piece glued into the appendage side first. The whole appendage was then glued on with 3M 77. I determined to also use some 5 minute epoxy at the inside of this joint but not until the majority of the carving was done. You do not want to run into hard glue when carving foam, especially in a tight hard to reach area like this joint. ** (See the note about this on pg.45)

Viewing

An important skill in sculpture and modeling is viewing the entire work carefully and from all angles as you work.

You want to compare lines, mass, shapes, and proportions. One tool that really helps me do this is an old department store display fixture that rotates slowly. This old turntable is perfect for viewing a foam sculpture. I can sit in a comfy chair with the maquette at the same attitude as the work piece and rotate both of them comparing and stopping as new things come to mind. Setting work on a turntable for review is always a good Idea.

So many sculptures have only one good view and most have a bad side. Try your best to get all views to be at least interesting and always shoot for multiple elegant compositions.

A turntable stand will help you do this task and I recommend using it often.

Work Lines

The form looks pretty much like the layout drawings and is ready to rough carve. The block has everything but the right side wing. The one flat side will allow us to set it on the bench and slice away without it rocking too much. You can see the relationship to the layout drawing is pretty good and the proportions seem adequate. It is time to start into some carving and get the forms roughed in.

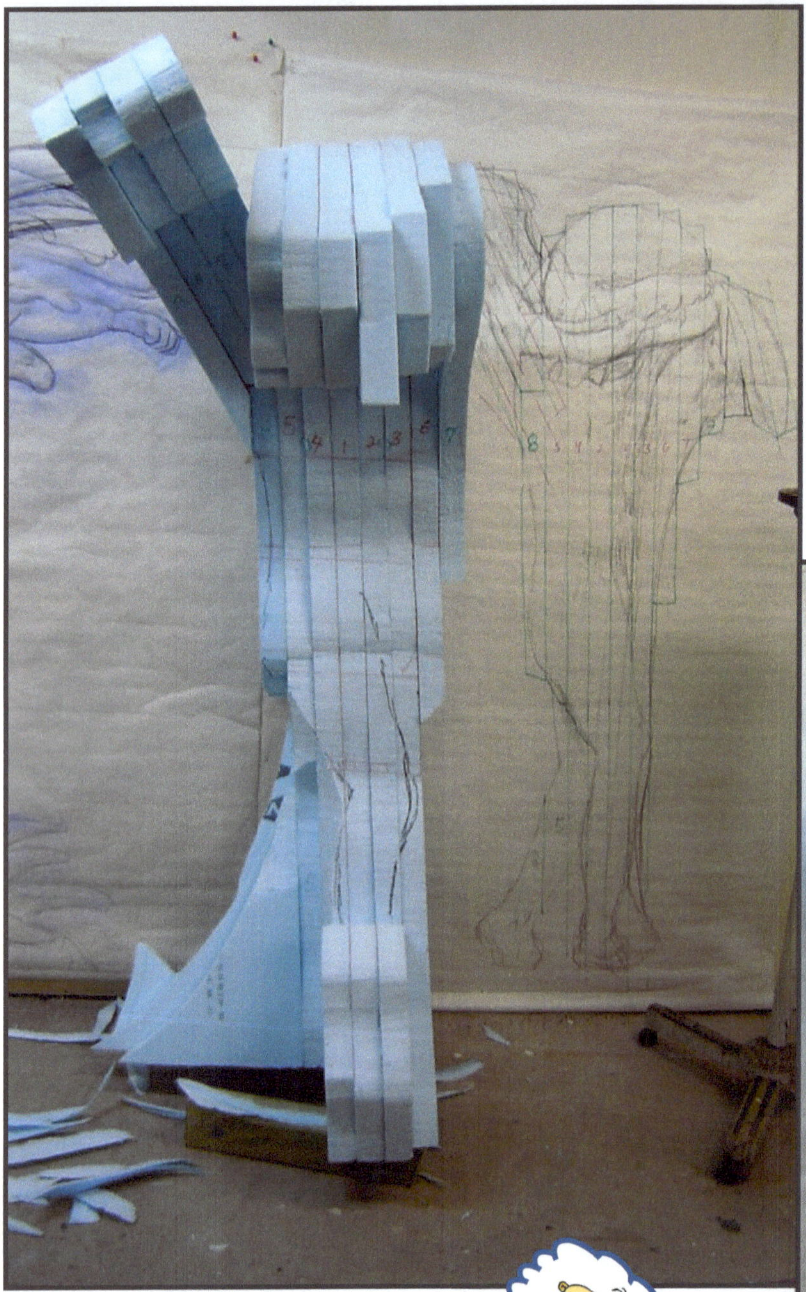

Before we start cutting it is a good idea to get as many work lines on here as we can. We step back and view them carefully to make sure we are happy with proportions and line relationships to each other.

The buttocks were readily created by cutting plank 8 right to this line. Now we will carve down in the end view and need the "wide line" of the back region. The front leg is sketched on and various other details noted, and compared to our maquette.

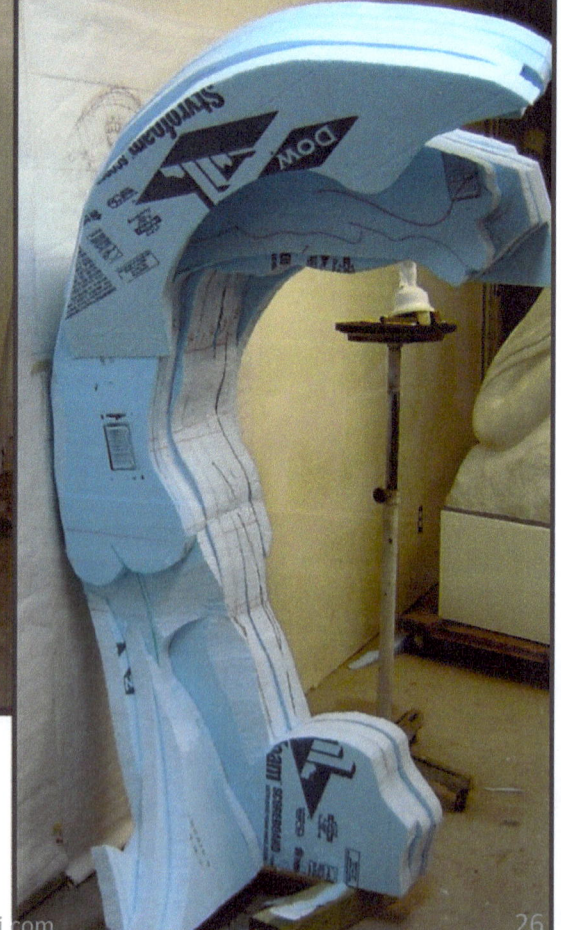

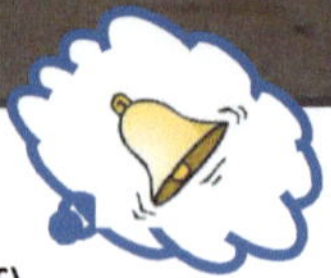

Are we good to go?   (a bell goes off)

The Craftsman's Internal Bell

Any time you are going to make a major move that is hard to turn back from, you should get a brain jolt. You're about to jump over a precipice and the bell goes off.

-Did I check everything?

-Am I sure of my direction?

-Is there anything else I should deal with before I go?

When You're about to change processes, make a mold, paint a part, cut into a big piece of stock, or do any operation that can't easily be undone just pause and review your work plan to make sure you have left nothing out. Think down the road and consider what mistakes could be avoided. This has helped me countless times as I recall disasters and set backs from former projects.

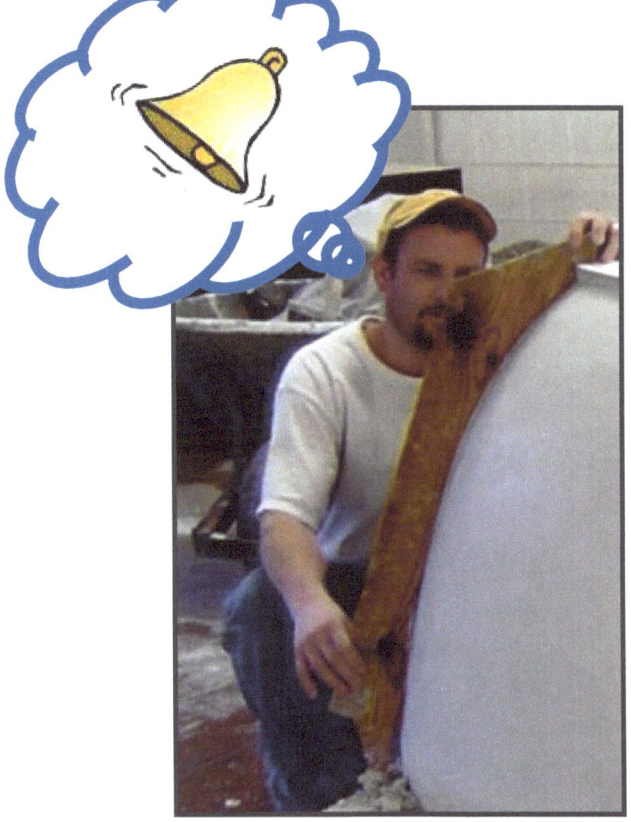

Even simple efficiencies save you time, like considering all that can be done with the piece in the current position. Are there any more operations that can be done in this position before I move it again? This simple thought process can save countless hours of rework and set up time.

When you see the bell icon in this book it is a good place to review your moves and options!

Major Hogging

At this point major bulk is carved away to get a better look at the proportions and distribution of mass before adding on the left side appendage. Hogging helps you make decisions about where and how to add pieces to get the form where you want it.

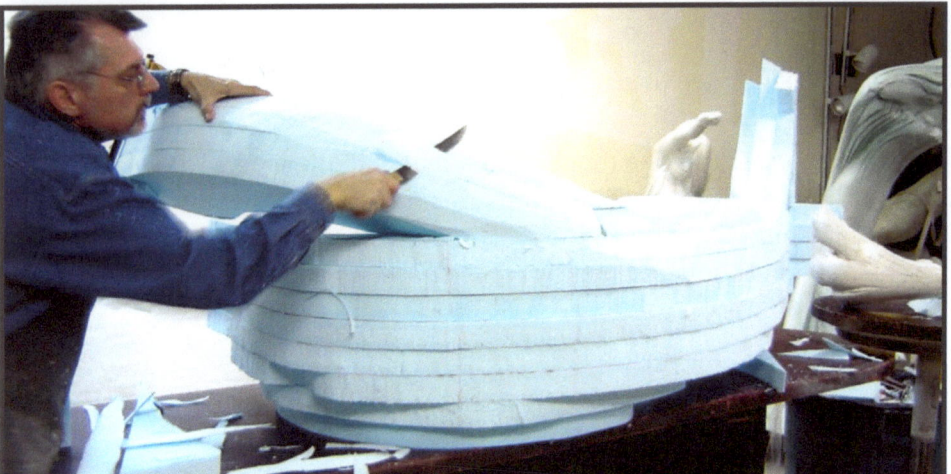

Your maquette is in constant use to help you make decisions.

How to hold this thing while you carve now requires a bit of invention.

The base planks protrude at right angles. This facilitates clamping to the bench and makes it stand up well so we aren't continuously knocking it over.

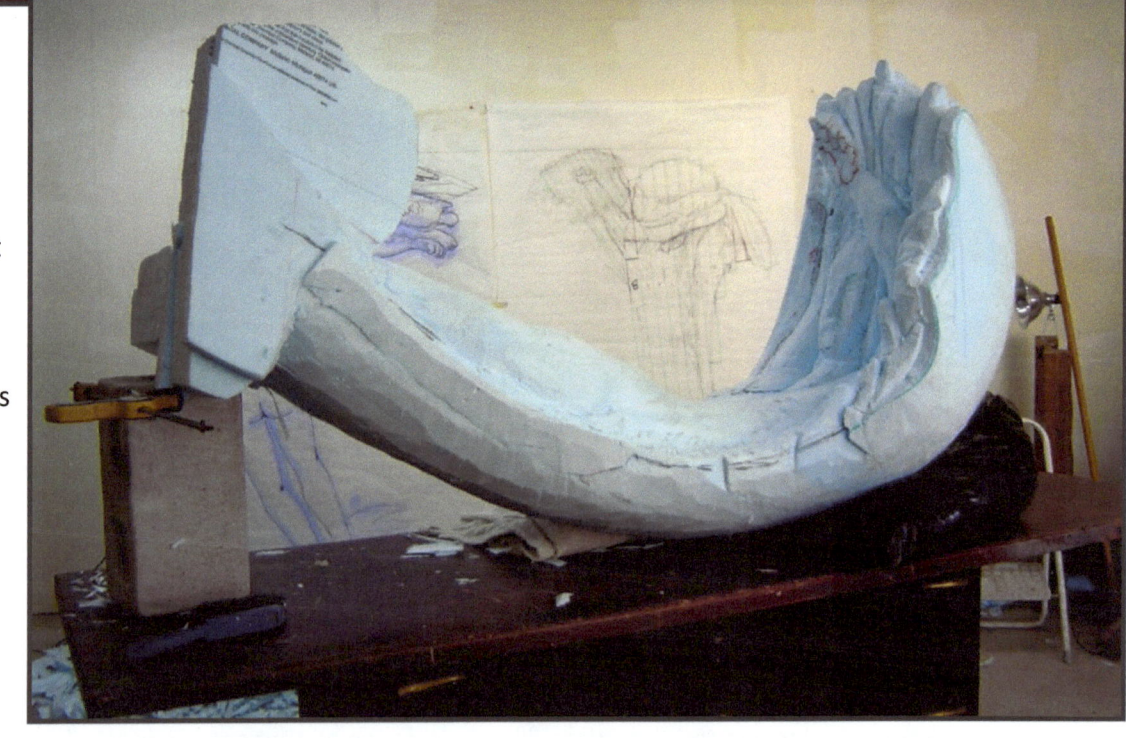

You do not want to begin carving any *detail* until you are pretty sure that all you need has been added to the block. This job is a lot of looking and figuring out. I cannot stress enough how important it is to leave any area which is questionable with flat 90 degree surfaces that will enable adding on material. It is a major pain to add once you have carved away and rounded surfaces. A bell should go off if you have any doubt about having enough material and you are about to carve off the last flat surface!

Templating with Plastic Film

Here is an easy way to transfer a line or dimension to a foam plank. A piece of clear plastic film is pinned to the work or drawing and a line traced on with marker. The film is then pinned to the plank stock and the pounce wheel used to transfer the line. For this section you can see the step down required from plank 7 to the next outboard plank on the drawing. You draw the outline of the next piece directly on the model noting the maquette as reference for placement. Then do the plastic film trick.

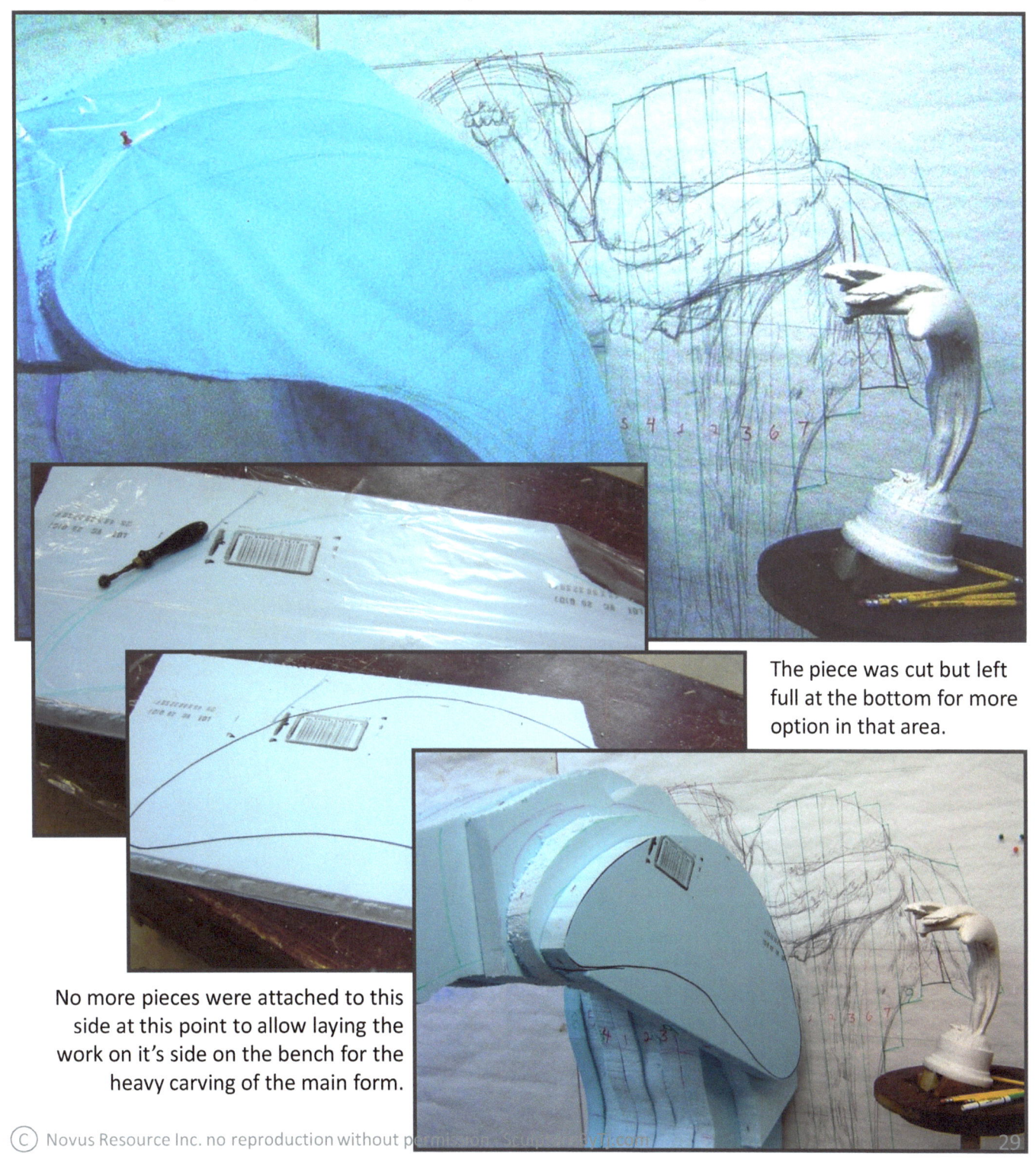

The piece was cut but left full at the bottom for more option in that area.

No more pieces were attached to this side at this point to allow laying the work on it's side on the bench for the heavy carving of the main form.

Adding On

The last appendage requires that you position the planks with a wedge so that the major finished surface would be within one plank. The wedge section was bigger than one thickness of foam and harder to cut out with ease. Since the wedge would be underneath where surface was not critical, we opted to make slices on the band saw and stack them together to achieve the flat surface. Some of the top of the plank was sanded away at the same angle. I did this so I would not run into the wedges when carving down to the surface. All was block sanded flat and prepped for gluing.

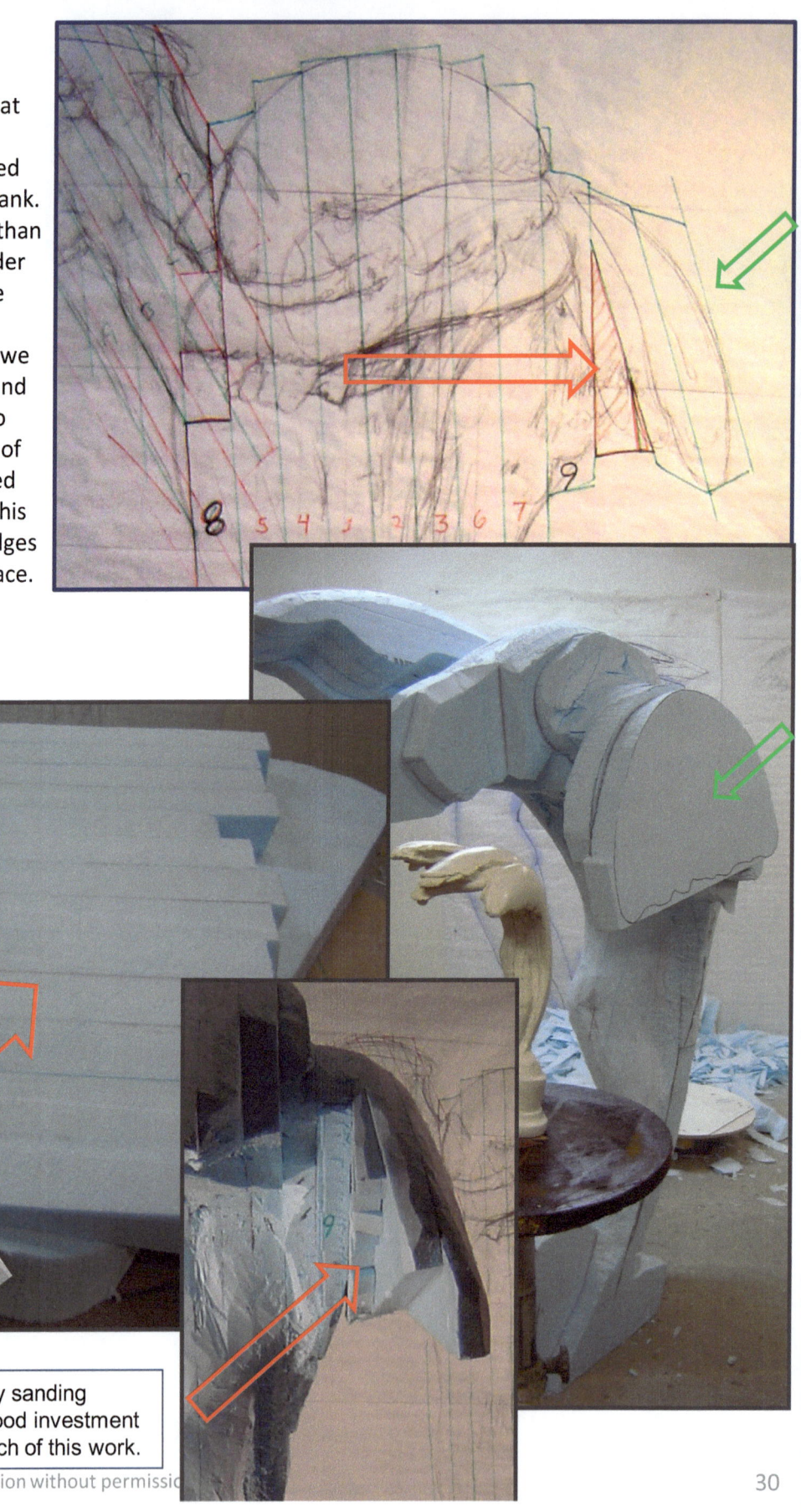

Angle sanded here

An auto body sanding board is a good investment if you do much of this work.

Adding On-

Plastic Film Technique

The plastic templating process was used for this addition by looking at the maquette and drawing a line on the plastic which has been pinned on the piece. This allows us to see through the proposed piece to forms beyond and view the line from the other side. Do the pounce wheel perforation on the board stock and retrace the line for cutting like before.

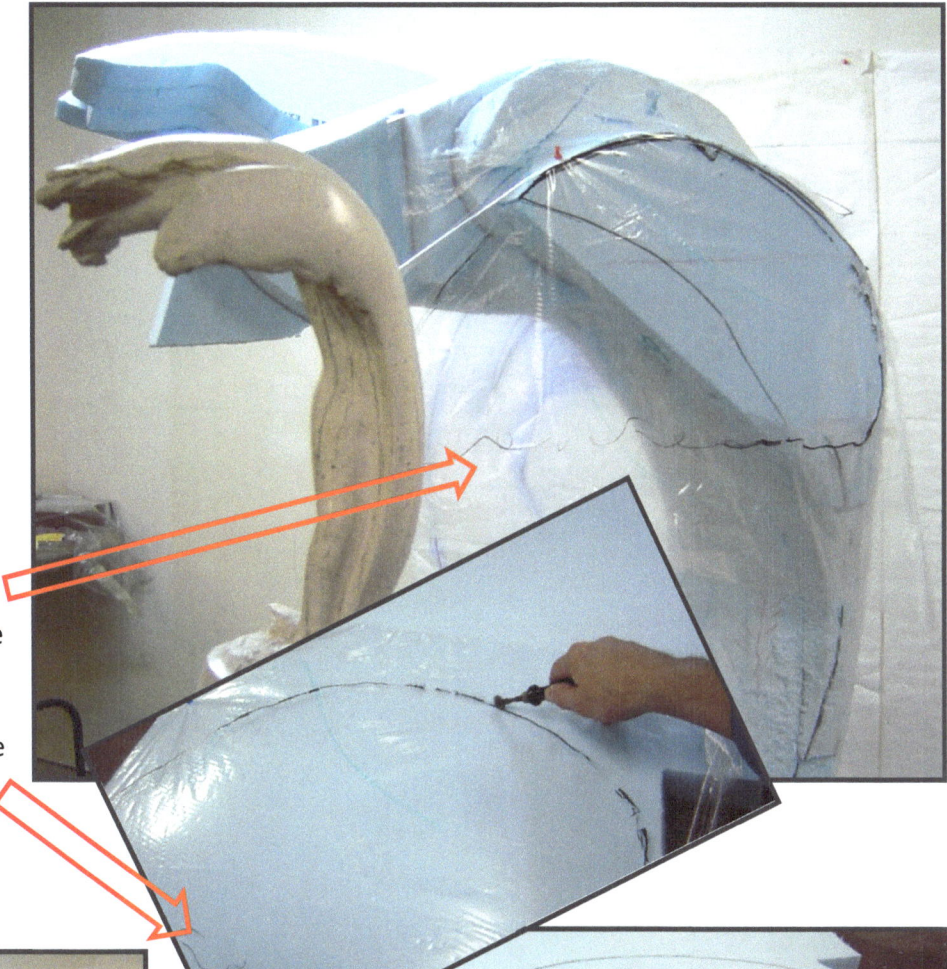

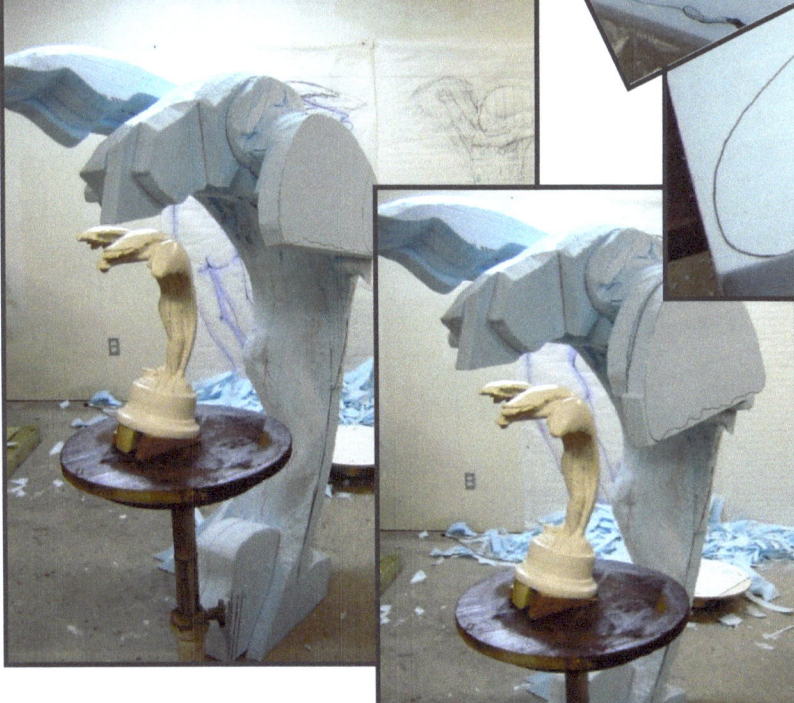

We determined a healthy amount of stock for the lower edge, cut and glued the blanks.

The second piece was just made a little longer to give even more carving stock and all was glued up with 3M 77.

Minor Additions

Here are some areas where the decision to add material was made a little later in the process, after the carving is under way. Often a larger version of a piece will present opportunities of it's own and you will want to use the new scale to the advantage of the work. Just remember, it is harder to add once the flats are gone.

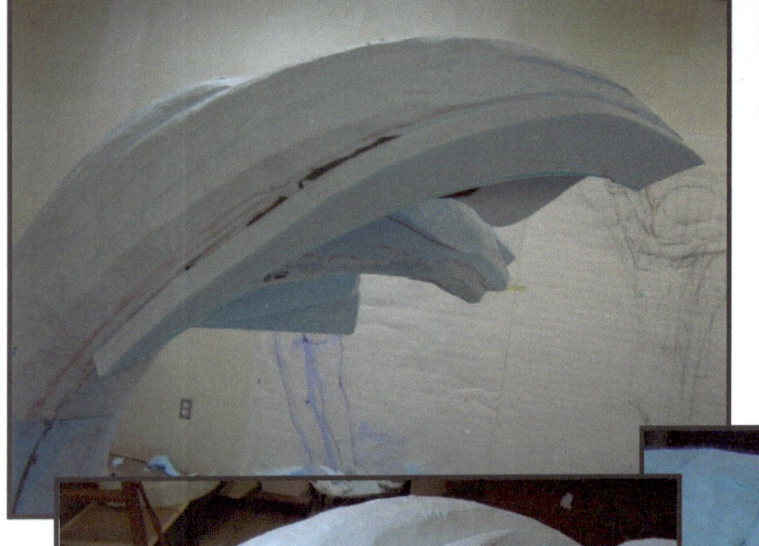

If you must make a change after carving, cut down or sand a flat spot to glue a new block into.

Fit the block carefully and make a right angle corner to fit to, if you can, for strength. The plastic template trick helps get a piece the right shape to fit here in this crevasse.

A Loose Piece - For Detail Work in Limited Access Areas

On this project I determined (after carving was well underway) that I needed more material in this area where the arm stretches out. It is covered here to give you the technique of creating a separate detail and leaving it removable during the carving process. This is extremely helpful when there is a lot of intricate detail in an area that is hard to get hands and tools into. This area is not flat, however and we will have to cut the back of the new piece to match the curve. This is done by using a cardboard or foam core template to match the piece up well.

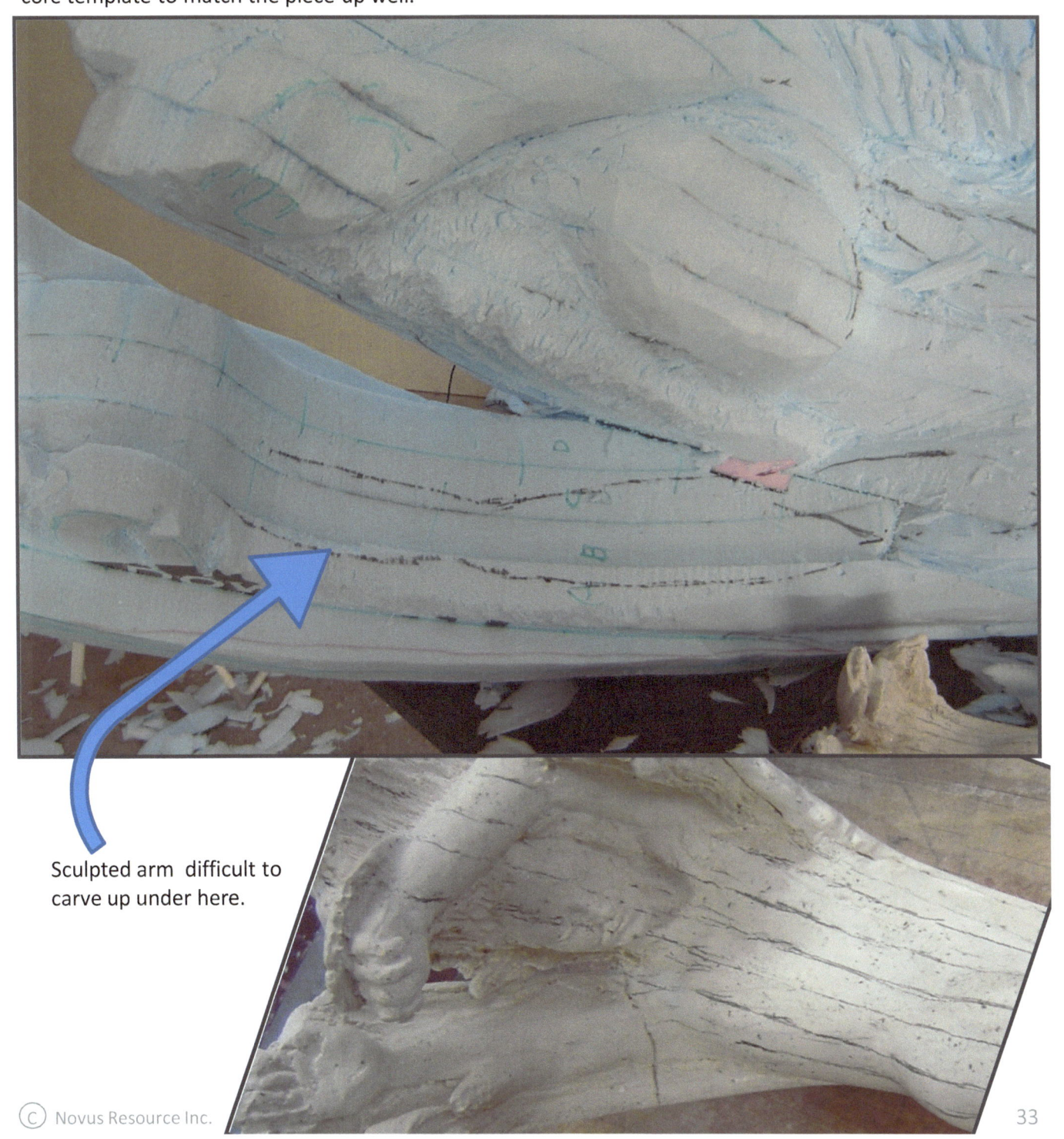

Sculpted arm difficult to carve up under here.

A Loose Piece–
Templating the Area

Here the back side of the piece needs to match the curvature . Use paper, cardboard and/or foam core to create a template that matches this surface perfectly. This is most easily accomplished by cutting something close, setting it up against the surface and using a compass to mark a line exactly parallel to the surface. Then cut your template to the new line and repeat this process until you fit spot on. If your piece is short or the area is really complex , you can make it from multiple pieces and just tape them together. Here an old piece of a sign did the job.

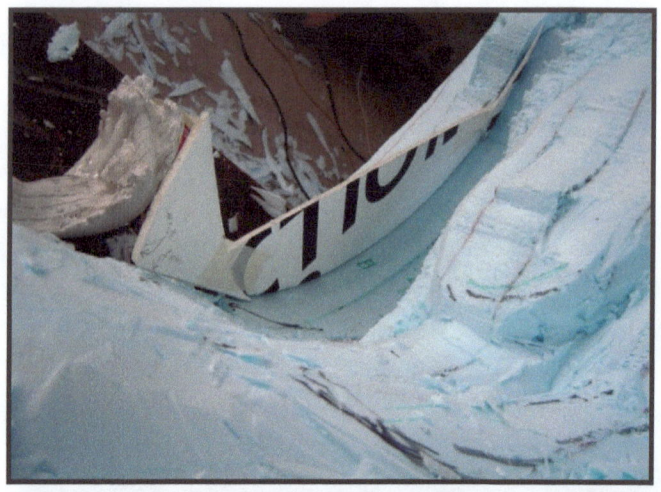

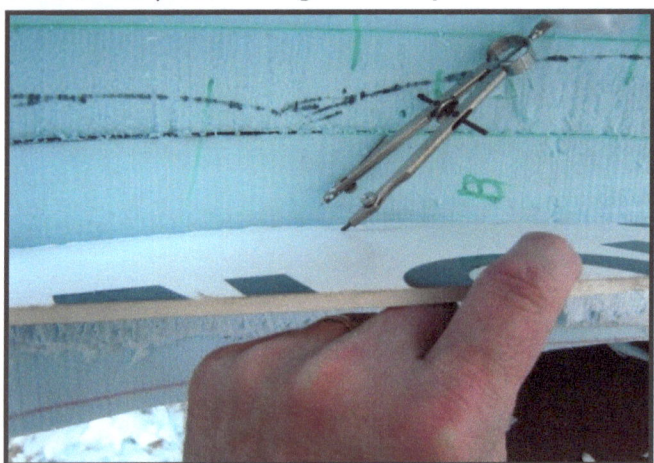

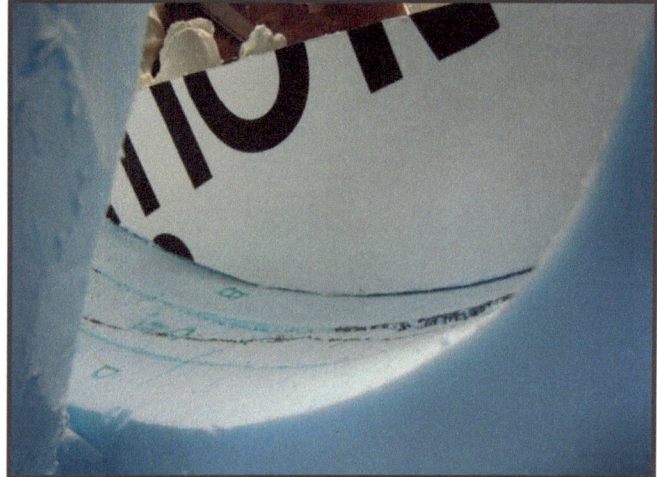

Now take the funky template and cut a piece of stock to get the "add In" started. Here you see the first cut piece fitted into the area. It will need to be 2 planks wide, so we make another and fit them together. Glue them to each other while in place to give the best fit possible.

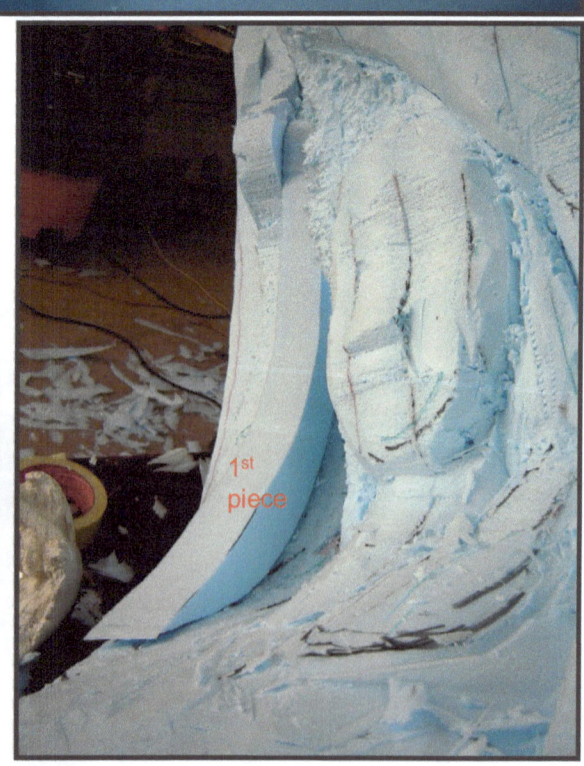

1st piece

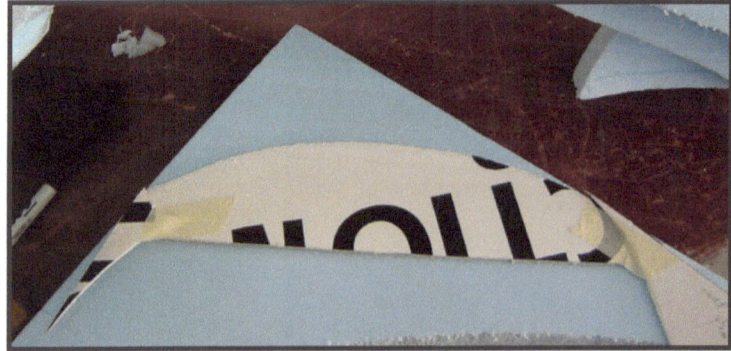

I save odd pieces of material like this so I have stock in all thicknesses and rigidity to use for templating.

Loose Piece- Adding in Pieces

Two pieces were laminated while fitting in place to create the stock blank for this arm section. The band saw was used to cut to the lines that were scribed in place to define it as an arm. (This one is tough to see, but look hard).

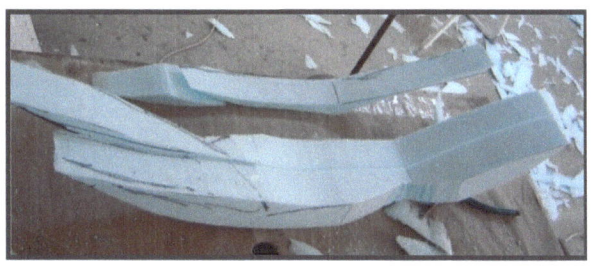

The block cutting technique was used. Draw views on two sides of the blank, cut one side, replace the cut piece. (Pins are good or two sided tape). Rotate 90 degrees and cut the other line.

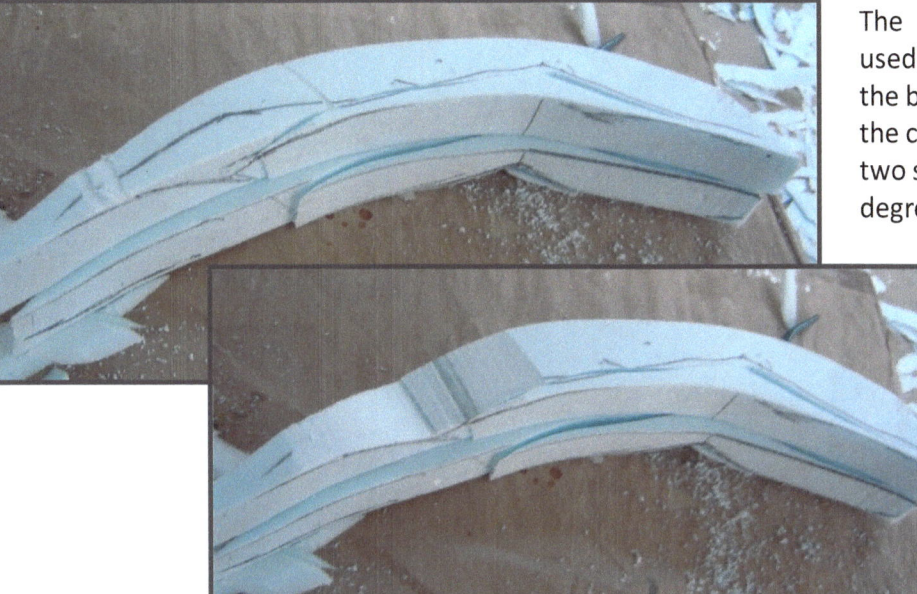

Replacing the cut piece keeps the block in tact and allows you to see all the lines. After the second side is cut we remove all the extra.

This "cut and replace" technique gives you most of the form definition. The piece is now marked for carving the surface.

Here you see it after some carving, still a loose piece.

A Loose Piece- Fitting and Blocking to Facilitate Carving

Creating all the detail in this upper hand would be extremely difficult in between the other forms. The solution is to make it a loose piece, enabling the detail carving, and fit the loose piece into this area. With the piece removed it is much easier to carve the details around it as well.

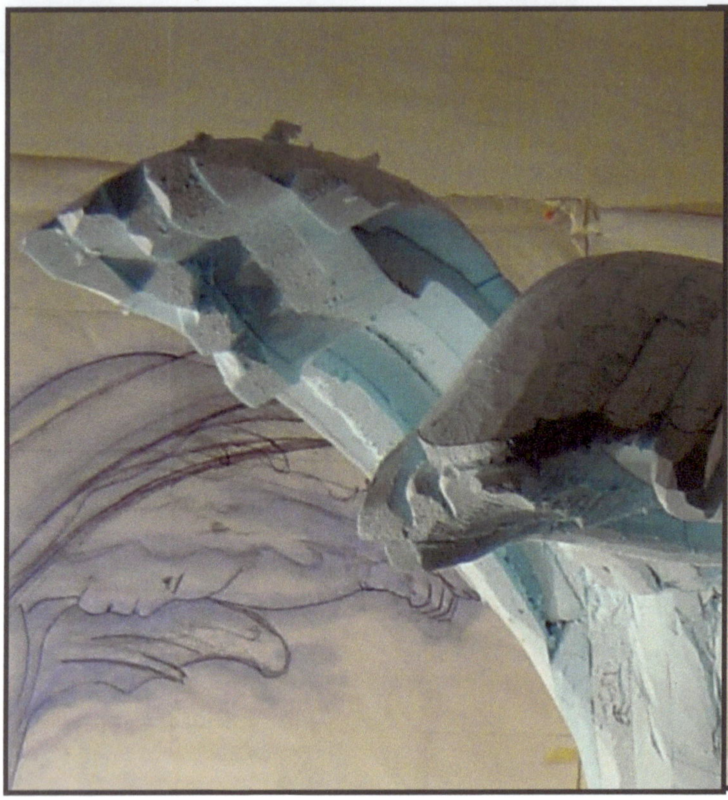

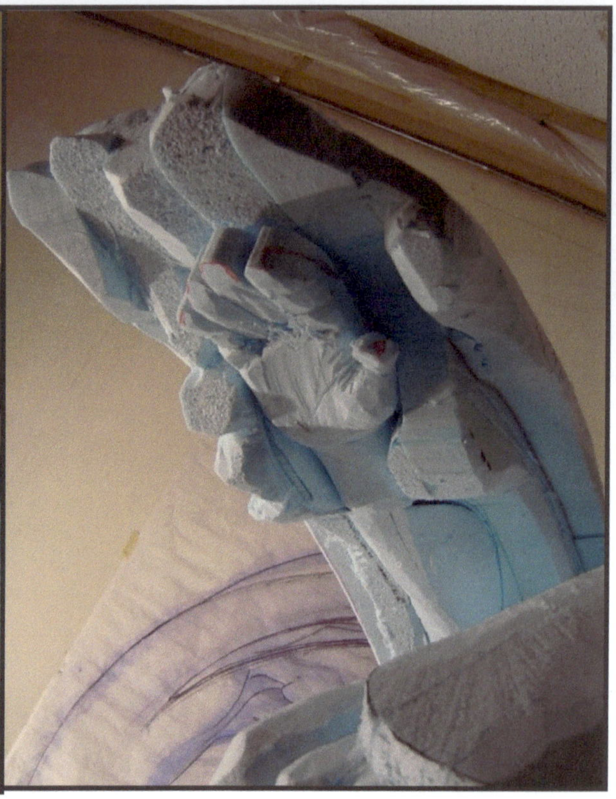

Trace the outline (palm up) and cut out the hand from flat stock. Then look at side views and sketch in details for further cutting and carving. (finger bends, joints, palm lines) A little block carving helps you see these shapes and forms. You locate it to the main block on a fairly flat intersection on the back of the hand.

The back is left flat (fingers un-carved back here) until you see how to fit it into the surrounding forms, and how to carve them.

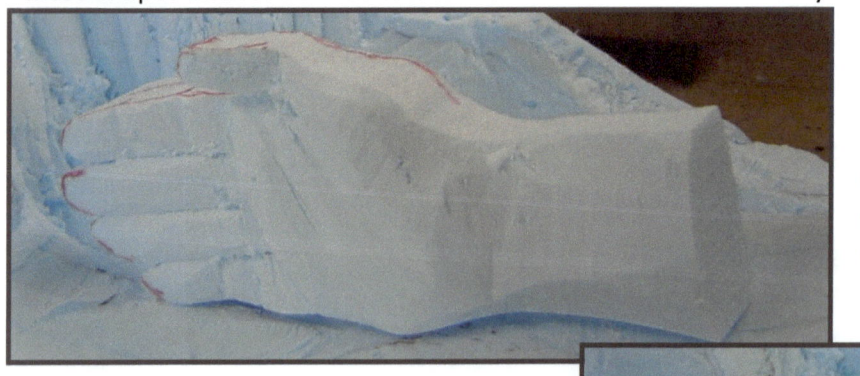

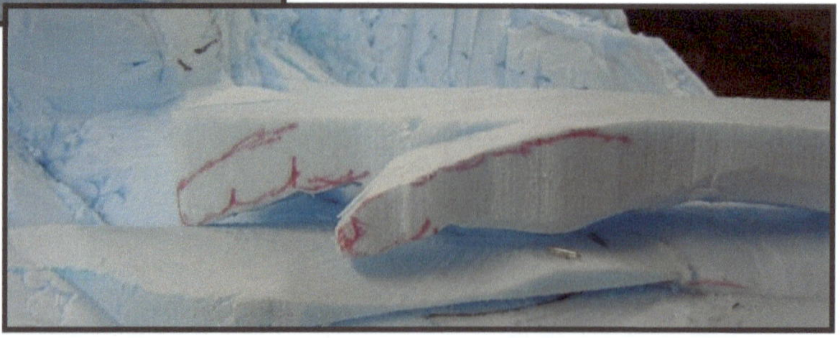

36

A Loose Piece- Fitting and Blocking to Facilitate Carving

Now trace around the piece and cut away material from the main block. Go back and forth between the two areas until you get a decent fit and the piece is nested nicely.

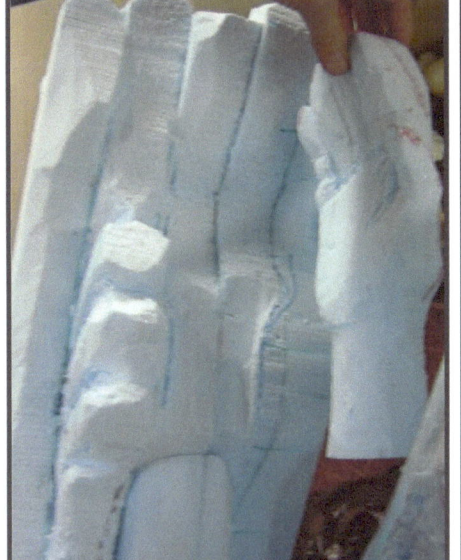 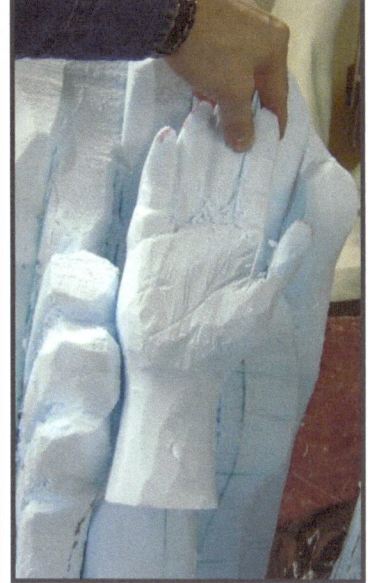 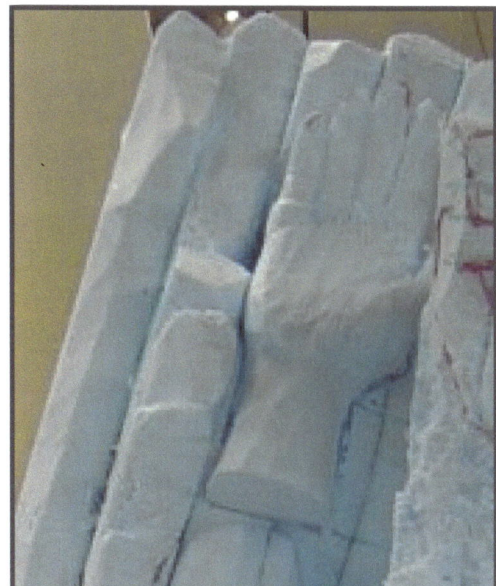

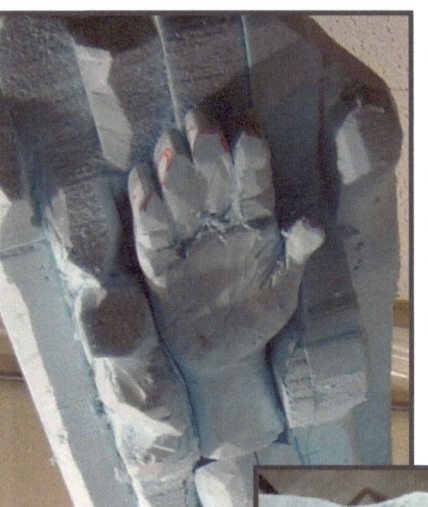

Leaving the piece loose really helps get in around it to refine surrounding details. In this case I was also fitting this piece to the rest of the arm down below. There was a lot of thought about how to make all the pieces assemble with as few seams as possible in the least obvious places.

You can see some of my lines for detail work and proposed ways to join the pieces.

Nice thing about a loose piece is an option to add to it or do it over.

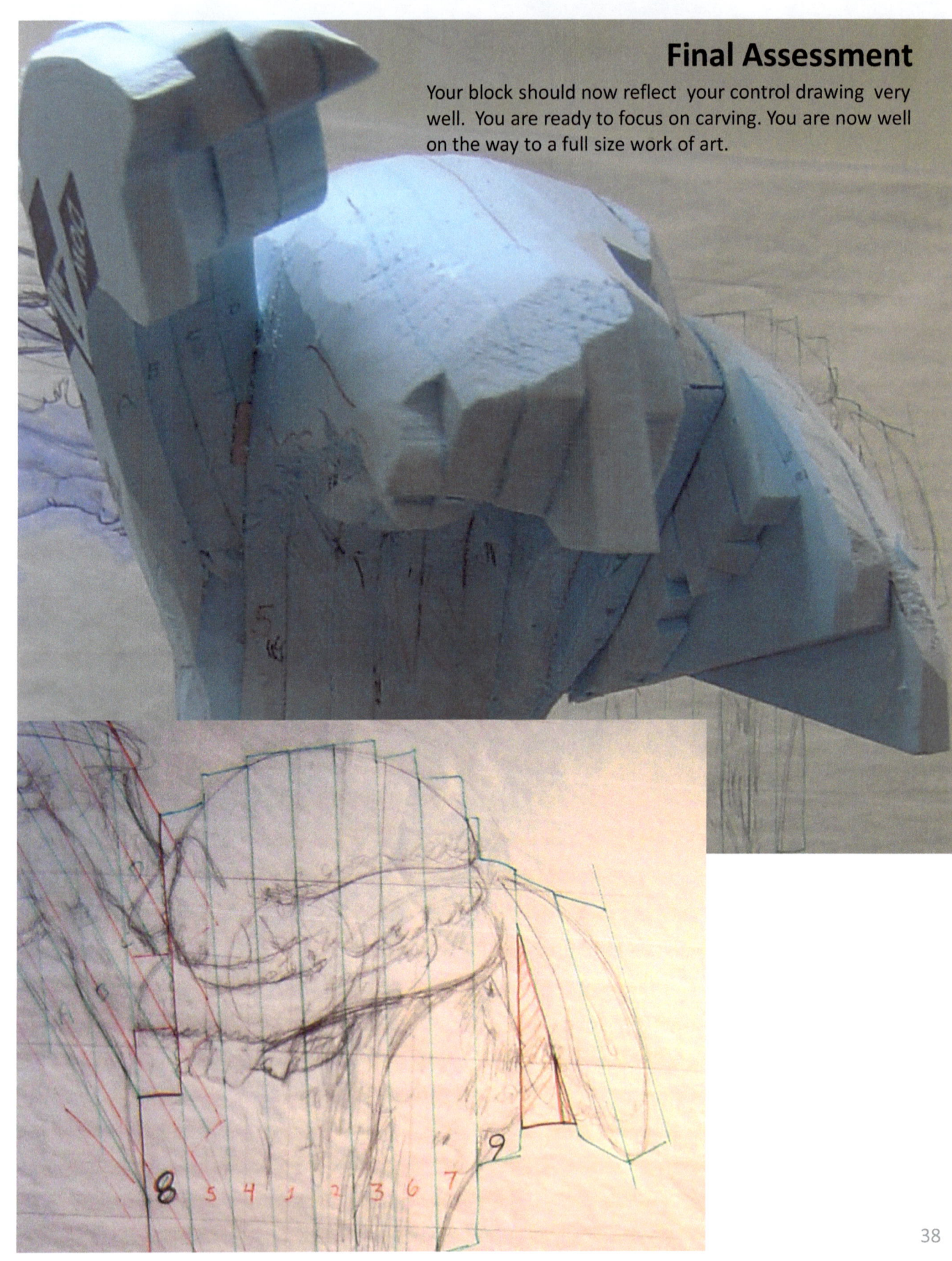

Final Assessment

Your block should now reflect your control drawing very well. You are ready to focus on carving. You are now well on the way to a full size work of art.

Not Confident Yet? A Simple Project in Foam - Relief Sculpture

Here is a simple relief piece that will introduce you to working with this material and process. Making a relief uses all the same technique as a 3D piece, but it is far less complex. I took my favorite photo of the *Impacted Male* and projected it as a pattern for a relief sculpture. The image transfer technique is the same as the 3D layout and block, but in relief there is only one view. The construction is just two panels. The photo was projected on a wall to the desired scale via data projector. The Plastic film trick is used to collect lines. (See Page 29).

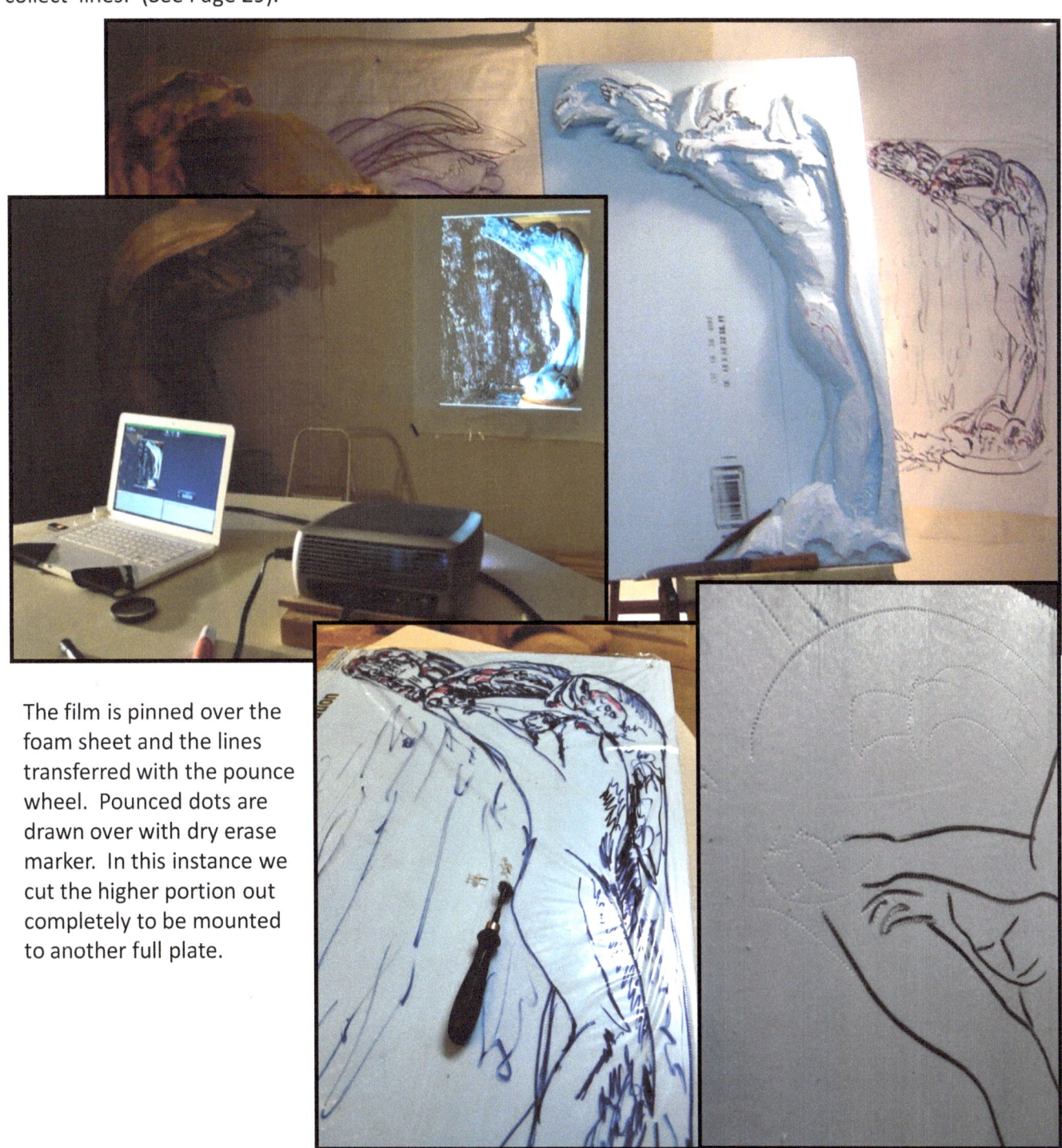

The film is pinned over the foam sheet and the lines transferred with the pounce wheel. Pounced dots are drawn over with dry erase marker. In this instance we cut the higher portion out completely to be mounted to another full plate.

Relief Piece – Developing a Surface

Draw on the surface with the dry erase markers and then cut to your lines. You want to refine your lines, then carve to them carefully. If you define the highest areas in one color and use a second color for the rest you will have good indicators. On this relief piece the red lines are at the highest points. Some are ridges to be carefully cut and some are topographic high points that we do not want to cut into while carving contours. We cut the ridges first and determine how far down to go with adjacent areas. **All the forms are drawn on all the time** until they are clearly visible from the carving.

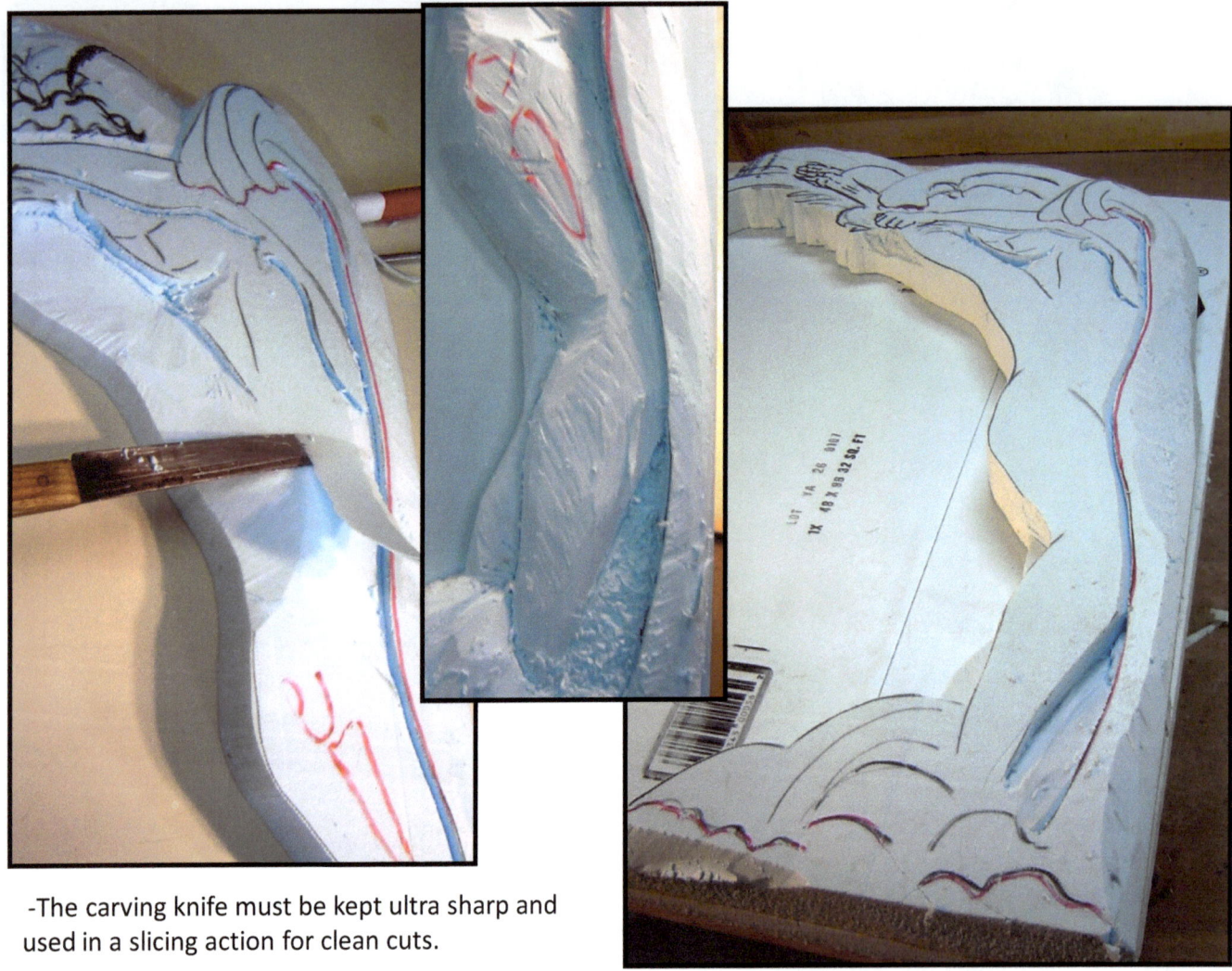

-The carving knife must be kept ultra sharp and used in a slicing action for clean cuts.

For sharp line detail use an exacto. Slice to your line and do a second 45 degree V cut. Then to bring down the surface elevation you can slice up to this groove with the big blade, pushing it just to your V cut. Some times you want to cut a line down into a surface just to preserve it while taking material off the surface. In this example you can see how the thigh puddle has been redrawn, after slicing, to lower the surface. Control is maintained with line and planning. Much more information on carving technique is in book 2 but it is important to understand the way we sneak up on a surface to create good drawings and use them to block surfaces.

Surface Development in Steps - (Sneaking Up on it)

Developing a surface means carefully constructing it while we keep it under control. Your layout drawing represents the data you will use to do the construction. Carving requires that we protect against removing material accidentally. Sneaking up on the surface is the prudent way to protect the high spots and refine the detail. This set of illustrations show a section (dash lines) through the relief sculpture at different stages. Starting with lines, cutting sheet blanks into sections, then carving down major forms, and finally finishing the surface. This process is the core of both carving and enlargement.

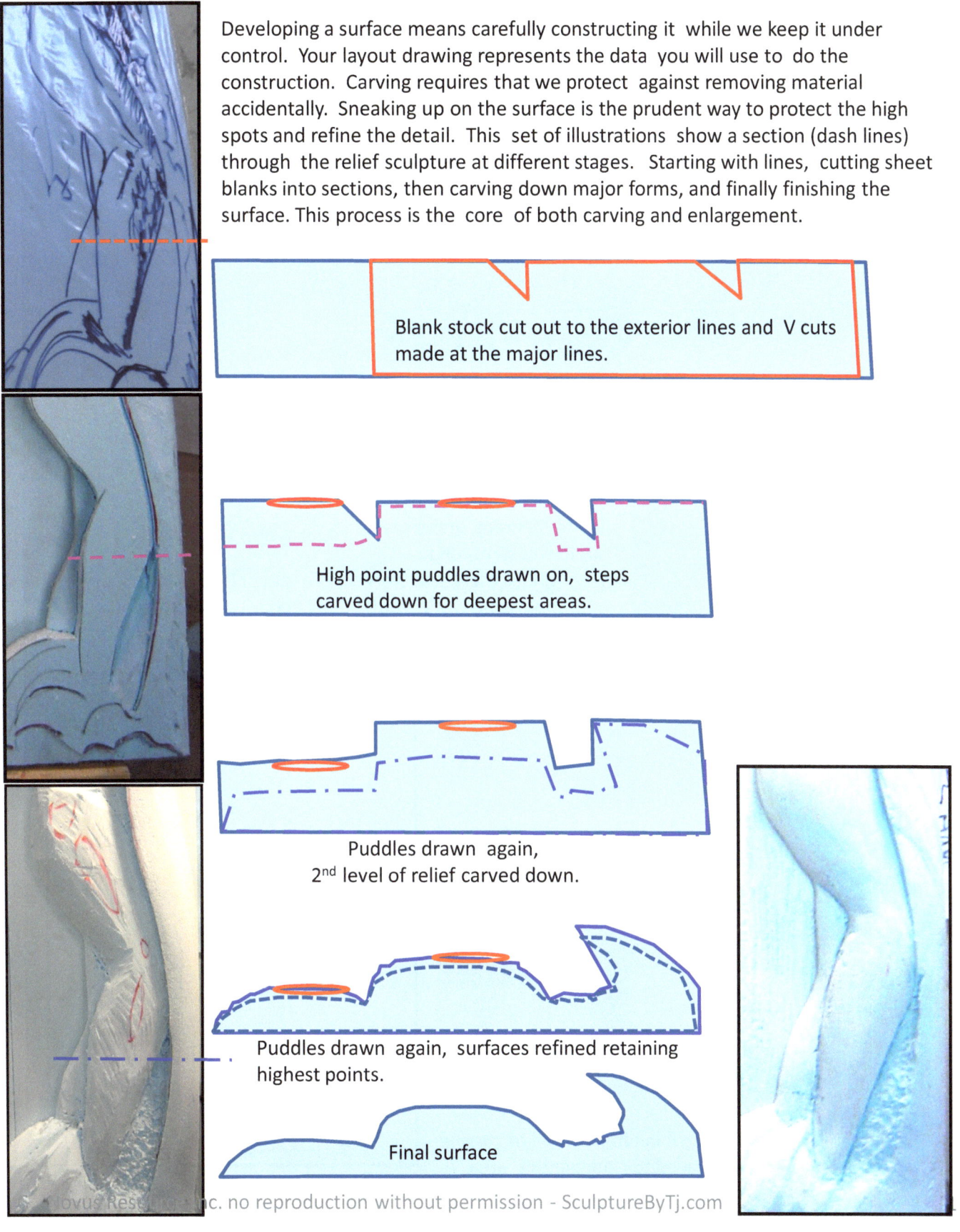

Blank stock cut out to the exterior lines and V cuts made at the major lines.

High point puddles drawn on, steps carved down for deepest areas.

Puddles drawn again,
2nd level of relief carved down.

Puddles drawn again, surfaces refined retaining highest points.

Final surface

Next Steps

The piece is now enlarged and blocked in. The next step is the carving of details, then comes the stone coating process. These two steps are illustrated in separate books available at:

www.SculptureByTj.com

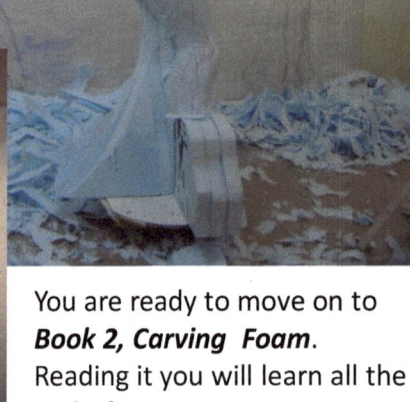

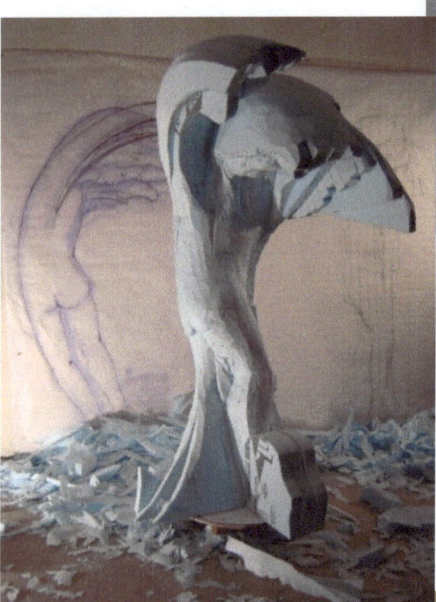

You are ready to move on to ***Book 2, Carving Foam***. Reading it you will learn all the tricks for very easy creation and refinement of forms in this low cost material.

Tj continues the visual story on the same piece and explains each operation as he works, with points about tools and techniques. ***Carving Foam*** also covers options for finishing your project .

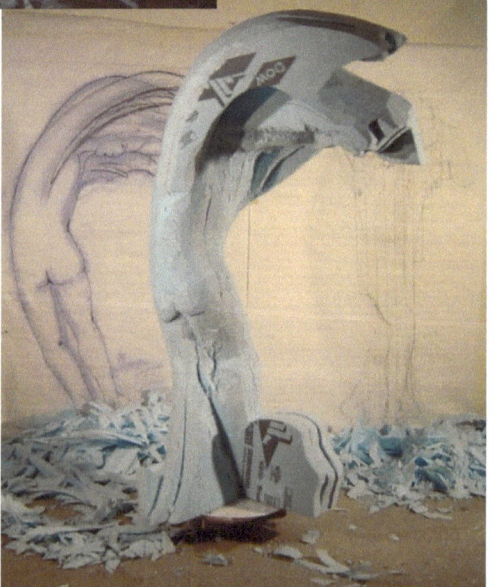

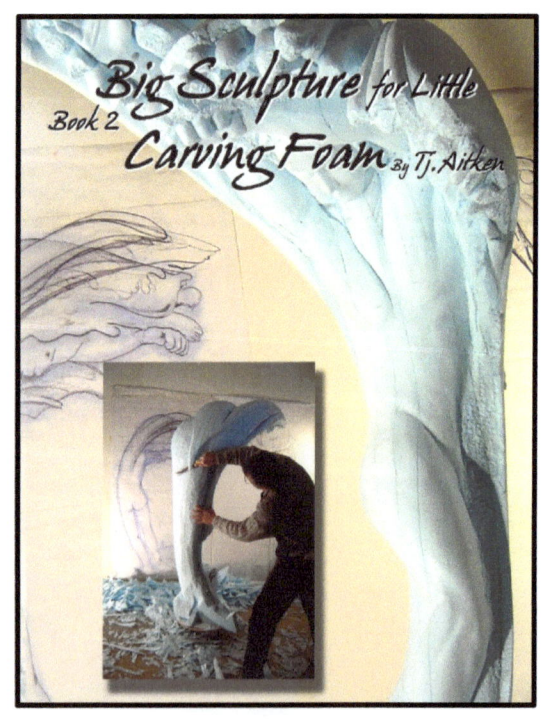

The base has not been discussed but the process will be the same. You will piece it in after the major carving is done and we no longer need to clamp in this area.

42

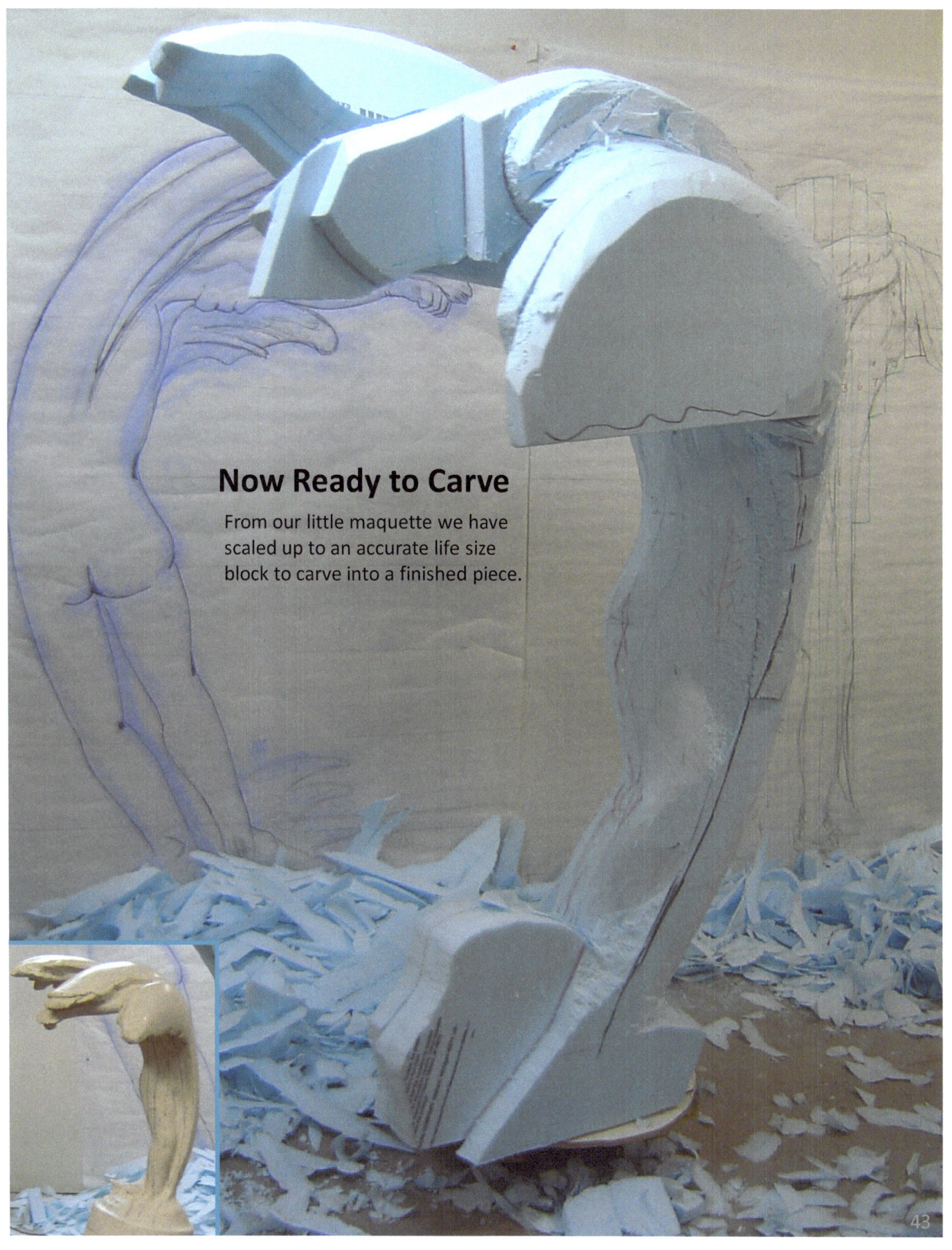

Now Ready to Carve

From our little maquette we have scaled up to an accurate life size block to carve into a finished piece.

About the Art Work

Impacted Man is from an installation called *Major Impact*. It has been under development since 1997 when a group of maquettes were done as studies for the piece.

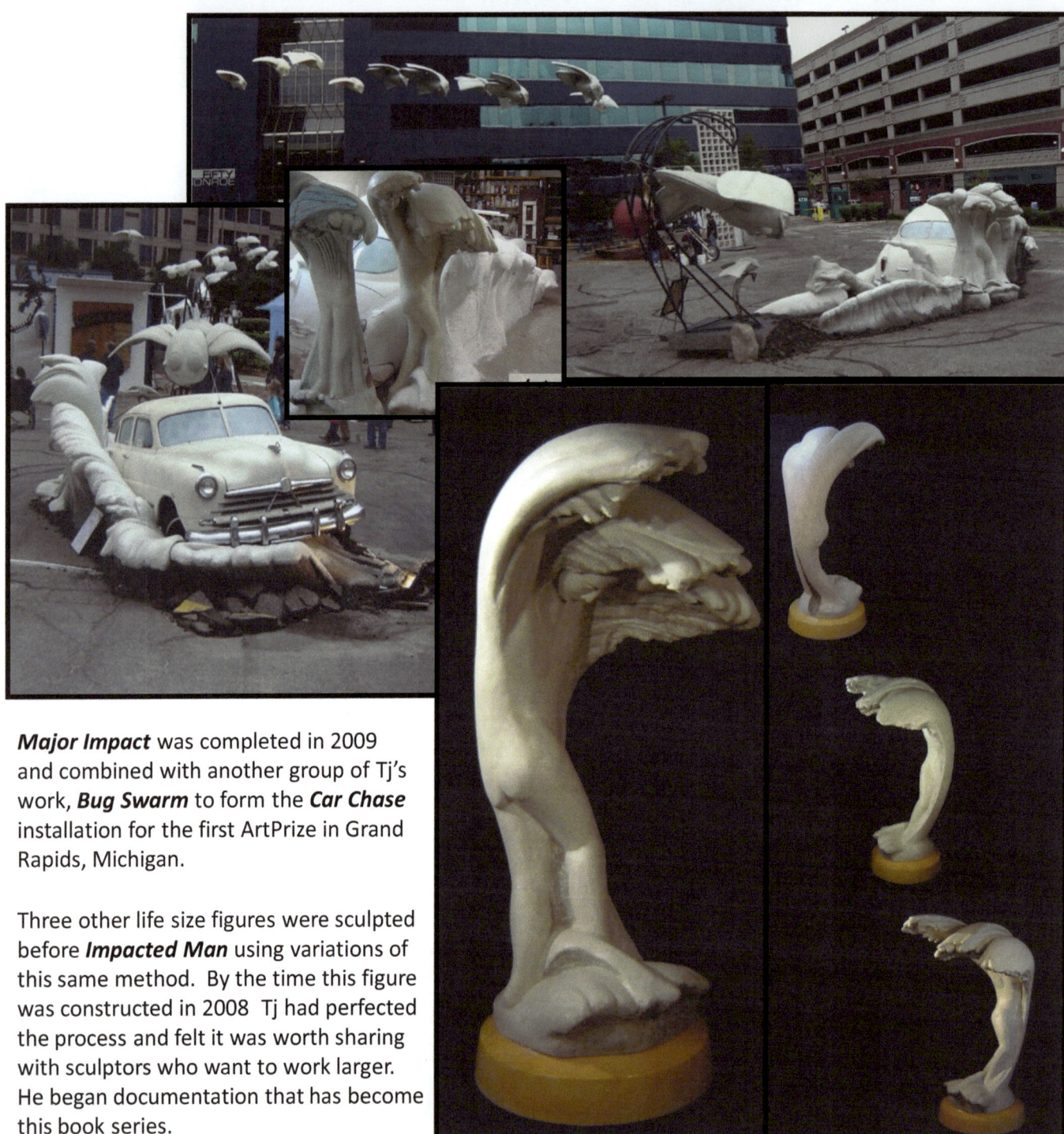

Major Impact was completed in 2009 and combined with another group of Tj's work, *Bug Swarm* to form the *Car Chase* installation for the first ArtPrize in Grand Rapids, Michigan.

Three other life size figures were sculpted before *Impacted Man* using variations of this same method. By the time this figure was constructed in 2008 Tj had perfected the process and felt it was worth sharing with sculptors who want to work larger. He began documentation that has become this book series.

The Appendage Story!

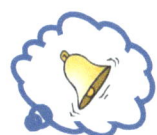

My craftsman's bell wasn't loud enough! This appendage joint was problematic throughout this build. At one point during coating I was carrying it through a doorway and whacked this appendage on the sill. I added glue to the crack but it had been weakened inside. Fast forward one year: *Impacted Man* is stone coated and finished. I was bringing it into the studio returning from a regional show. (Two of us carrying it). The long arm created by this protruding block cracked, and I took it off. It broke cleanly along the joint. I drilled two ¾ inch holes (positions indicated in red) right through the whole form and mudded in dowel pins with 5 minute epoxy. Both interior sides of the joining area were troweled with epoxy as well. The appendage was replaced and the surface finish was reworked. I V cut the surface and added extra strong glass filled cement to the

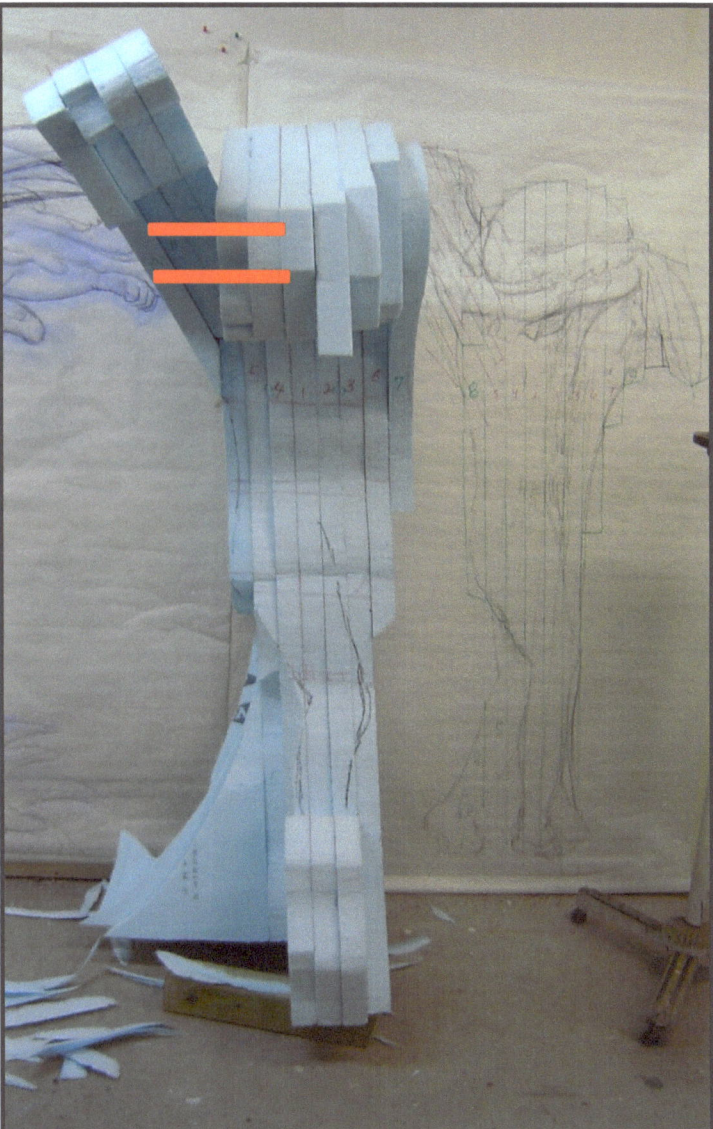

patch joint and a bit of extra material to the surfaces around this joint. Fortunately these materials match up and the repair is not visible.

In perfect hind sight I now see the proper method would be to add those dowel pins and extra glue at the point when carving is finished and the exterior coating is about to be applied. At that point in the process I would be done with carving and out of danger of running into hard glue. The patching of a couple of dowel holes with foam plugs is a simple task before finishes are applied, unlike the repair job that I had to do.

This incident also led to a stronger outer coating material that would also have prevented the break. More on that in Book 3.

Oh well, another one for the "Lessons Learned" file, but it's to your gain.

About the Author

Tj Aitken   Installation Artist

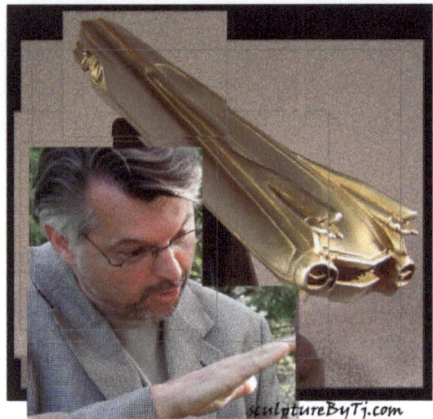

Tj does sculpture installations, workshops and consults on creativity management with his company Novus Resource. He writes on art themes and for "how to" books. His sculpture theme:
"The Impact of the Auto on Human Society" is his passion.

His installations include: Grand Rapids Public Museum ArtPrize 2010, and ArtPrize 2009 (top 25) - *Sculpture in the Square* Installation Troy Ohio, Solo Show Logsdon 1909 Chicago 2008, Marshal M. Fredricks Sculpture Museum biennial show award 08, *Velocity*- International Invitational Minneapolis MN 2008, *Eyes on Design* top art prize Grosse Pt. MI 07. He has spoken on quantifying aesthetics at the Harvard *Front end of Innovation* conference, the Innovation Network, and the Creative Problem Solving Institute's annual conferences

Tj was a design director for a fortune 300 automotive company. He worked in Europe in the 90's setting up design studios and managing projects. He has lectured world wide, training thousands of engineers in managing aesthetics. He holds design and process patents and his materials have been translated into 5 languages. He now applies his expertise as a design director and prototype build manager to the world of sculpture. He can be contacted through his website at: **www.sculpturebytj.com**

www.ingramcontent.com/pod-product-compliance
Lightning Source LLC
Chambersburg PA
CBHW040750200526
45159CB00025B/1836